from
FETTERS
to
FREEDOM

With Best Wishes
From Nóra
May 1997

from FETTERS to FREEDOM

The Inside Story of Irish Jailbreaks

by
Mícheál MacUileagóid

ISBN 1 901005 05 4

Published by
SÁSTA
Ashton Centre
5 Churchill Street
Belfast BT15 2BP

3 5 7 9 10 8 6 4 2

Cover Design, **Mac Mahúna** Digital Design, Belfast

Typeset in Belfast by Sásta

Printed in Ireland by
Colour Books, Baldoyle Industrial Estate, Dublin 15

Acknowledgements

A book such as this one would have been impossible to compile without the help and advice of countless individuals. Not only did I have the aid of modern technology but I also had access to the unlimited help and opinions of some 'old fogeys'. I am indebted to them all.

One of the problems with a book such as this is that somewhere along the line someone will feel that they have been left out. The nature and size of the subject has made it virtually impossible to include every escape. In fact some of the attempted escapes and even the planning involved, with those which did not come to fruition, may have been just as exciting as those which did eventually succeed. Hopefully I have demonstrated the varied nature of some of the most memorable escapes which have taken place since Ireland has been colonised and I am grateful to everyone who has helped me achieve this.

There were many people who from time to time added their own reminiscences to the story and made corrections where they thought they were necessary, they are too many to name here. I am extremely grateful for the help and encouragement I received from Joe Baker, Liz Curtis, Paul Liggett, Brad, Ann, Ronnie, Cíarán Flynn and the staff at AP/RN.

I am also thankful for the additions by those people who did not wish to be named. Thanks also must go to the staff of Central Library Belfast, the Linenhall Library, Belfast and staff of the National Library of Ireland for directing me to some source material.

I am especially indebted to Jimmy McDermot and Susan McMahon who helped me fine tune the manuscript and delete any 'meanwhiles', 'howevers' and 'therefores'.

Particular thanks must go to Martin Meehan, Cahir O'Doherty, Alex Maskey, Liz McKee, John McMullan, Joe Barnes, Gerard Burns, Frank Quigley, Terence Clarke, Pat McGeown and Gerry O'Hare for taking the time to allow me to interview them. Their contributions to the script were essential in creating the authentic version of events.

Mícheál MacUileagóid

CONTENTS

Easter Monday was the day of days for them. They had heard the glad Alleluiah in the chapels, telling that death had been conquered and the grave made to give up its dead.
They were dead - was there to be a call to life sped to them, even there in the dark Sepulchre of Slavery, amid the corruption of sin and crime? .... They pass from Fetters to Freedom.

The Irishman, June 10th 1876

Introduction

A stalemate has been reached on many occasions in the prison code regarding the treatment of Irish political prisoners. Conditions cannot be too harsh otherwise it will provide ammunition for propaganda and provide further sympathy and support for the prisoners' cause or *raison d'être*. Similarly the conditions cannot be too lax otherwise the prisoners will escape, thus, furthering their cause and gaining sympathy or support for the prisoners, their communities, their families and supporters. The government has to find, therefore, that fine line between harsh incarceration conditions, while at the same time provide as humane a regime as possible according to international laws.

Throughout the penal history of Ireland special arrangements have been implemented to deal with rebels. Special rules and conditions were introduced to either placate these prisoners or punish them. All those who opposed Britain's conquest of Ireland were regarded as criminals or subversives and as thus the government and her allies felt morally justified in punishing them. Up until 1922, when the Treaty was signed, most of the jails were controlled by Britain. Following the Treaty however Ireland was divided into two distinct administrative areas. The British Government retained control of the industrial north-east, while a Free State was established on the rest of the island. A bitter battle was soon fought between those who did not wish to abandon the six counties and those who had accepted the terms of the new treaty agreement. The British sided with those who were pro treaty and before long a civil war was raging throughout the country. The old jails which were used by the British administration, such as Kilmainham, Mountjoy and Arbour Hill, were reoccupied and the regime was further augmented with the Curragh camp and Portlaoise. In the north of the island new prisons were also built to hold the latest batch of prisoners — the most notable being Long Kesh (which was renamed the Maze), Magilligan and Maghaberry.

As the political disagreements raged, prisoners continually played a main role in the resolution of the national problem. There has constantly been an argument as to whether or not the prisoners from either side were political prisoners or criminals. These issues have culminated in prison protests, hunger strikes and escapes in every decade since the first colonisation of the island. At one end of the scale the government introduced concentration camps for their prisoners while at the other end of the scale isolation units were developed. Prisoners were sometimes treated as prisoners of war, under the rules drawn up under the Geneva Convention. At other times they were treated in the harshest way possible. An example of this was the imprisonment of the Fenian, Jeremiah O'Donovan Rossa. During his imprisonment in England he was chained to the floor like an animal. To do this in modern times would raise such indignation in human rights courts that it would be virtually impossible for the British government to get away with it. Furthermore the financial ramifications would undermine the economy. By 1990 the prison security bill to guard four hundred political prisoners at the Maze was running at £40 million per year. The staff outnumbered the prisoners three to one at the prison, thus undermining the strategies for low cost prison management.

The development of prisoner management came about through Britain's need to control her colonial prisoners. The policy of holding them on prison hulks before dumping them en masse at Van Dieman's Land or elsewhere throughout her empire, eventually stopped and Britain was faced with the problem of trying to hold her hostages closer to home. In order to isolate the prisoners, many were shipped over to camps and prisons in England or Wales, until eventually the government believed they had developed their own top security jails in the north. The government in the South of Ireland soon followed suit and Portlaoise and Long Kesh became the scenes of the final showdown between the captive and the captor.

In modern times the prison crisis has raised its head repeatedly. With embarrassing frequency the prison escape has been at one extreme, while the hunger strike has been at the other. The government has continually played a cat and mouse game with its prisoners, in trying to find the solution to the ultimate problem in Anglo Irish politics - How do you come to a compromise in incarcerating or subjugating people who do not believe you have the right or authority to do so in the first instance? The British government have consistently tried to effect such a policy from the earliest times of colonisation.

Modern theories of control and inmate management have been studied by the British government since it was forced to abandon the policy of using the penal settlements. Control of both prisoners' minds and movement were studied but the theories put forward relied on creating small self-contained groups of prisoners who will obey prison staff. Political prisoners or prisoners of conscience in Ireland have consistently formed groups amongst themselves and elected representatives, both inside and outside of their prisons. It was within such groups and through their highly organised friends on the outside, that the seeds of escaping grew.

Many escapes of prisoners throughout the world, have proven that the desire for freedom is a common human yearning. Some escapes have been remembered for their ingenuity. These include the man who laid a piece of sacking in the corner of a field, soaked it in water and then sowed oats on it. When these were a few inches high he hid himself under the sacking and began to crawl slowly away through a field of growing oats. So effective was his camouflage that warders could not find him until they put a dog on the scent. Others included the many prisoners who escaped in disguise. Some left as priests, lawyers, visitors, or even warders themselves. When these techniques did not work the prisoner resorted to cutting through bars, climbing over walls or tunnelling under them. As time went on and technology developed we witnessed even more daring escapes, some using helicopters, others boats and even 'tanks'. In every instance the people who control prisoners have had to constantly update their holding techniques to stay one step ahead of the escape committees. Sometimes they failed.

This publication is an in-depth study of the escape phenomenon as highlighted by those who have proved to be the most consistent and professional escapers in the history of civilisation — the Irish political prisoner.

The removal of the Fenian prisoners from Dublin Castle to Mountjoy prison.

1. Time to go

The concept of the hero escaping from the clutches of his captor has been handed down to many students of Irish history, orally. Indeed many of the Irish myths and legends came to be in our possession because of the richness of this oral history.

One such story was that of a northern leader from Donegal named Red Hugh O'Donnell. Elizabeth I was in the process of subjugating the Irish at the time and had been met with fierce resistance throughout Ireland. The English settlers had established a stronghold in the City of Dublin and its surrounding area. Sir John Perrott was the Crown's Deputy in Ireland and when Red Hugh O'Donnell was a mere boy of fifteen years of age, he was arrested and taken to Dublin Castle where he was held hostage.

The O'Donnells ruled most of Donegal at the time and the English government believed that a deal could be struck with that clan for the return of their son. Dublin Castle was surrounded by a deep moat which could only be crossed by a bridge. The entrance to this bastille was guarded night and day by English soldiers. In December 1590, after nearly three and half years imprisonment the chance to escape presented itself to the youth.

A new Deputy called Fitzwilliam was appointed to Ireland and he put an elderly soldier by the name of Maplestone in charge of the jail. Maplestone was not in the best of health and was often absent due to illness. Weighing up the risks involved, Red Hugh decided to use this opportunity to get out of his enemy's clutches. He had already been in contact with a friend called Fiach McHugh O'Byrne. O'Byrne was another opponent of the English and he contrived with Red Hugh to ensure that the escape would be successful.

Red Hugh and some other prisoners managed to acquire a rope ladder, and one night after supper the prisoners were together waiting on Maplestone to get the keys to lock them up for the night. They knew that the soldiers took a break around 7.30pm whenever the night duty began. They also knew that around the same time their friends would be waiting outside in Castle Street. They quickly tied the rope to the window bars and then, after squeezing through the window, climbed down the rope to the ground below.

Once out of the jail, they then had to get beyond the city walls before the alarm was raised. In order to prevent anyone coming out of the castle, Red Hugh jammed a piece of wood through the rings which lowered the castle door thus delaying the soldiers. They met up with their friends in the adjoining street and made off on foot through the city gates, which were still open at that time of the evening. The party never stopped until they were ten miles south of the city's walls. After a short rest they headed further southwards to the mountains in an attempt to reach Glenmalure and the territories controlled by Fiach McHugh O'Byrne.

Meanwhile the alarm was raised at the castle and the soldiers had shouted to the townsfolk to release the wood from the front of the castle gates so that they could give chase. The English who were on horseback made swift progress, as opposed to the escapees who were on foot. Red Hugh decided to call on the help of a family friend called Feidhlim O'Tuathail but O'Tuathail did not prove to be a good friend. While sheltering at his castle Fiach was contacted and was informed of Red Hugh's whereabouts. The weather worsened and before O'Byrne could reach Red Hugh, Feidhlim handed him back to the English. Red Hugh O'Donnell was behind bars at Dublin Castle again, but those others who accompanied him on the escape reached the safety of Glenmalure never to be caught again.

After reviewing the safety procedures, a new and stricter regime was imposed at the castle. This time Red Hugh was held in a tower on the south side of the castle. He was put in irons and chains which were fastened to the walls every evening. This time however he had the company of two other enemies of the Crown. They were Art and Henry O'Neill. Art had escaped once before and it wasn't long before he and Red Hugh were conspiring to escape yet again. Although still a teenager, Red Hugh showed determination and ingenuity, which were just two of the talents which eventually led to him becoming a leading figure in Ireland's opposition to the English conquest.

Red Hugh set up a line of communication with his friend Fiach McHugh O'Byrne. He told the prisoners that he would be sending a messenger into the Castle yard to negotiate the purchase of several horses. Red Hugh and the two others decided to escape on that day by gaining entrance to the sewers which ran under the castle. On

New Years Eve 1592, with the use of a file which they had smuggled in they cut their irons. Luck was with them as Maplestone took ill and did not check their leg irons as usual. The prisoners were able to cut through their irons from early afternoon. Then with a makeshift rope of cloth, they were able to let themselves down through the Castle's drainage system, which led from the top to the bottom of the Castle. Before they could get into the hole however they had to discard their cloaks.

They came out the other end into a channel of water. It was a bitter cold evening and the snow was falling quite heavily. They headed to the prearranged spot where Fiach's messenger was supposed to meet them with horses to take them to the safety of Glenmalure. Unfortunately there had been a blunder made and, for some reason or other, he could not get the four horses on that particular night. They decided that they would have to try and reach the mountains by foot.

Art however had had an accident earlier that evening. While escaping a rock had injured his foot and he was already limping badly. Nevertheless they decided to continue. Darkness fell quite quickly and as they hurried along the road through the mountains they lost Henry. They later learned that he had been recaptured and imprisoned.

The other three continued by the same route which Red Hugh had taken on his first escape. This time they were hampered by the freezing cold. Art began to falter, and after two days walking they stopped at the top of Glenreemore where they took shelter below a cliff face. Art's condition was becoming worse, and although the other two were not much better, they were determined to reach Glenmalure.

Red Hugh decided to send the messenger on ahead while he waited with Art. It was only ten miles to Fiach's fort and it wasn't long before help was on its way. The rescue party were horrified at the condition of the two brave young men. By the time they arrived both were buried beneath the snow, unconscious and frozen. They could not revive Art and he was buried where he died. A plaque marks the lonely grave to this very day. Red Hugh was in a critical condition and he was brought back down the glen where a doctor was assigned to look after him. Meanwhile word was sent north to the O'Donnell clan telling them of the rescue. Hugh O'Neill from Dungannon immediately sent down an escort to bring Red Hugh back to Donegal once he was well enough. Red Hugh lost two toes as a result of frostbite. He came back to a tumultuous reception hosted by his people and became one of the most revered heroes of Irish history for his gallant escape from Dublin Castle.

Not all of those who escaped came from the North, even though the latest escapes from British and Irish jails have featured Northerners. The same determination is common throughout all the escapes. Another famous escape had much in common with Red Hugh's adventure. This was in October 1922, when one hundred and forty one internees made off from Newbridge internment camp at the Curragh. This time however it was the Free State government who were in control of the prisons. There had been a sensational breakout the previous year in which up to fifty men had escaped, but on this occasion the tunnellers connected to an old sewerage drain at the Barracks. This time the internees' escape was heavily censored, and news of who had got away began to filter through to the respective families. The newspapers only covered the story briefly, due to a directive censoring press and media coverage of such events, and because reporters and editors relied on information being supplied directly by the army. As a result of these restrictions, the full story of many of these breakouts has never been revealed. For many other reasons, in the interests of the prisoners themselves, some escapes and escape plans have been abandoned or put on hold until a more suitable opportunity presents itself. Because of the nature of escapes and the constant need for secrecy, the full extent of these plans will never become public knowledge.

In the South, a government directive was issued at the beginning of October 1922, to all censors and editors of newspapers, instructing them what they could and could not write about. Supplied by the Army Publicity Department at Beggars Bush, Dublin it contained twelve directives, two of which dealt with prisons and prisoners:

> *MILITARY CENSORSHIP*
> *GENERAL INSTRUCTIONS*
> *1. The Army must always be referred to as the "Irish Army", the "National Army", "National Troops", or simply "troops".*
> *2. The Irregulars must not be reffered to as the "Executive Forces", nor described as "forces" or "troops". They are to be called "bands" or "bodies of men".*
> *3. Irregular leaders are not to be referred to as of any rank, such as "Commandant", etc., or are not to be called officers.*
> *4. No news as to movements of troops may be published.*
> *5. No news may be published as to the movements of newly enrolled members of the army, movement of foodstuffs, or trains, or transports of equipment for army purposes.*
> *6. Description of a military operation must not be published while the operation is still incomplete, for instance, an encircling movement.*
> *7. Articles or letters as to treatment of Irregular prisoners may not be published.*

8. The Censors are not to insert words of their own in any article submitted to them. Their business is to cancel what is objected to. They may, however, propose to substitute words or phrases, such as "Irregulars" for "Republicans", "fired at" for "attacked", "seized" for "commandeered", "kidnapped" for "arrested", "enrolled" for "enlisted".

9. Letters, news or articles dealing with proposals for peace, or negotiations with the Irregulars, should not be passed without submitting them to the Chief Censor.

10. The term "Provisional Government", should not be used. The correct term is "Irish Government", or simply "the Government".

11. All GHQ Bulletins from here should bear the date and time of issue.

12. Escapes of prisoners must not be published.

By Order
Army Publicity Department
Beggar's Bush, Dublin

Instead, newspapers depended on the official statement being issued.

Army Bulletin. 16 October 1922
TUNNEL DISCOVERED

On the evening of October 13, the authorities discovered a tunnel in process of manufacture in the Gymnasium, Wellington Barracks. There was a hole three foot square cut in the floor and a shaft sunk to a depth of about four feet, till it met the foundation wall at the gable end next to the Grand Canal.

The earth taken from the tunnel was stuffed into mattress covers and the flock from the latter was scattered about the floor. In the centre of the Gymnasium under another hole two hundred and eighteen rounds of .303 were discovered.

The Argenta Prison Ship which was moored in Belfast Lough in 1922.

2. Floating Bastilles

It is not generally known, but the practice of confining prisoners on ships is strictly modelled on the precedent of 1798, when not one but two prison ships were moored in Belfast Lough. Dr Steele Dickson, one of the Presbyterian reformers of the period and who is buried in Belfast's Clifton Street Cemetery wrote vivid descriptions of the living conditions on board the infamous prison hulk called the *Postlethwaite*. Arrested on the eve of the rebellion on 12 August 1798, he was placed on board this floating bastille.

> *On reaching the Quay of Belfast we found boats in waiting, embarked safely and soon reached our floating bastille......When we first came close to the hatchway we were met by a hot fetid steam, from the multitude below almost intolerable.Through it however we were obliged to descend and on reaching the deck found it literally crowded so that there was some difficulty in clearing a corner for us. This done we had to contemplate our situation which was truly unpromising.*

The lower deck, where the majority of the prisoners were confined for the greater part of the day was, according to his calculations *only four feet eight inches high, so that we could neither walk nor stand upright.* He continued. *"Many were obliged to lie in opposite directions, with their limbs intermingled, the feet of one range reaching to the knees of the other."* No bedding was provided and scores of men *had not even a straw between them and the hard planks when either sitting or lying.* Food was limited to stirabout made up of oatmeal and water for breakfast. Dinner consisted of a mess of beef or salt pork with the ship's bread *without vegetables of any kind or even a potato.* The only food utensils were the tubs and cans in which the rations were dished up and *many had to tear their food asunder like wild beasts.*

Under such repulsive conditions, then, was it any wonder that a desperate attempt would be made to escape. By late 1797 the *William and James* tender was moored in Belfast Lough with eighty-seven of the United men on board. On 3 January 1798, the prisoners surprised their guards in a coordinated attack. The guard at the time consisted of naval ratings and a detachment of Reay Fencibles. The watchword was 'Blood Blood.'

In the subsequent scuffle prisoners in the press room gained control of a rope ladder leading to the deck, but whenever all the men climbed it together, their combined weight proved too great a strain and the rope broke unceremoniously throwing the prisoners back into the hold. This frustrated their plans, and after a fight, two naval officers were wounded, the Naval Military Force, led by Lieutenant Elsmer, soon gained the upper hand. One prisoner, named Cassidy, was shot dead as he attempted to swim ashore. Several others who had been shot in the fracas were moved to the shore to have their wounds treated.

A huge clampdown was then brought into force and, although there is no written proof, it can be safely assumed that the conditions under which the prisoners were held became more restrictive as a result of the escape attempt. It is known that the Naval Force was doubled. This increase in troops was provided by another detachment of the Reay Fencibles who had been based at the Artillery Barracks, Belfast. After the defeat of the insurgent forces on the field, a further ship was chartered to take many of the prisoners who were held at Belfast. The naval records make it clear that the last ship was sent to replace a smaller previous vessel, and that she too was fitted with no means 'that may add to the ease of rebels held on board.'

Another attempt by Irish prisoners to escape occurred three years later. Two square rigged two deckers sailed from Cork harbour to the prison colonies of Australia on 29 November 1801. They were called the *Hercules* and the *Atlas*. By 29 December the *Hercules* was rounding Cape Verdes when the plans of the convicts came together. Shortly after 2.30pm the Captain heard the cries from the female passengers in the roundhouse. The majority of the soldiers and seamen were below deck having lunch. On deck were two guards and a helmsman. Upon further investigation it was discovered that the prisoners had overpowered the guards and had taken control of the quarter deck. Two weeks previous to this an informer on board the *Hercules* told the captain of a plan by the prisoners to mutiny but as nothing had happened immediately the captain had lowered his guard. The captain of the ship Luckyn Betts along with his chief mate, Aiken and the Commander of the guard Captain Ralph Wilson ran from their cabin to see what could be done. One of the convicts snapped a blunderbuss at Betts and Wilson but it failed to go off. Wilson immediately shot the man dead. Aroused by the sound of the shot the soldiers and seamen swarmed on deck and began firing at the convicts. The fighting lasted for fifteen minutes after which the prisoners began to lose control of the quarter deck. They were eventualy forced to take shelter below decks in the prison hulk. After forty five minutes the crew had regained control of the ship. Thirteen prisoners had been killed. One hour after the rising one of the prisoners, Jeremiah Prendergast was forced to kneel down on the deck where he was shot dead by the Captain. For the remainder of the voyage Betts kept the prisoners confined below decks. The result of this confinement was quite obvious once the ship reached Port Jackson, after a passage of two hundred and nine days. The prisoners were emaciated and filthy. Including the fourteen men killed as a consequence of the mutiny there had been an additional forty four deaths due to disease and hunger. Many of those who survived the voyage required immediate medical treatment. A Vice-Admiralty Court in Sydney found Betts not guilty of killing the thirteen mutineers. From charges arising out of the killing of Jeremiah Prendergast, he was convicted of manslaughter and fined £500, the court ordering that he should be confined in prison until the fine was paid. The Governor of the Colony granted him a conditional pardon and left it to the British authorities to decide if he was guilty or not. He obliged Betts to surrender to justice within four days of his return to England. No action was taken against him and Betts escaped punishment.

The prison hulks, were, at the time, the government's method of containing their convict problem. Jails up and down the country were only designed to hold prisoners for a short time before they were executed or released. The hulks were used as holding centres for convicts before they were transported to the prison colonies. With the development of prisons after the colonies refused to accept any more prisoners, hulks became obsolete. Conditions on board these hulks at times of political unrest became unbearable thus leading to public outcries and protest. Although conditions on board the first convict hulks in 1798 were well documented the government retained plans for the use of prison hulks at least as far as Northern Ireland was concerned, right up until 1972.

Sir James Craig was the first Prime Minister for Northern Ireland and was responsible for the introduction of the Special Powers Act. The original bill had nine sections: arrest without charge or warrant; internment without trial; flogging (repealed in 1968); prohibition of inquests; execution; use of depositions of witnesses as evidence; destruction of buildings; requisitioning of land or property; and prohibition of meetings, organisations and publications. The state of Northern Ireland was officially set up in June 1921. The Government of Ireland Act came into force on 3 May 1920. Prior to this there had been internment in the North at Ballykinlar, County Down.

Ballykinlar Camp was then divided into two sections each holding about one thousand men. The two sections were separated by barbed wire fences and manned

The Argenta Internees being transferred to Belfast Jail after their arrival at the Midland Railway Terminus, Belfast in January 1923.

sentry boxes. All the internees were Republicans. Orders were to shoot anyone trying to escape. Indeed, Jim Tormey and James Sloan were shot dead at the camp in January, 1921 and Alderman Tadhg Barry died under similar circumstances on 15 November that same year. Internment lasted until the signing of the Treaty on 6 December 1921, after which, the vast majority of internees were released unconditionally.

On 23 May 1922, internment was announced yet again. At first the internees were kept in Crumlin Road Jail, Larne Workhouse and a camp near Newtownards, but in June their collective destination became known - the prison ship *Argenta*. This ship was moored off the coast at Carrickfergus and visitors had to be rowed out to her. Later, internees were taken in handcuffed pairs to Larne to see relations or solicitors at the local RUC Barracks.

The *Argenta* was a US ship which was completed in 1919 at a cost of $150,000. As it was not required for wartime service it was sold to the Northern Government for £3,000.

The Ship was specially fitted out as a prison hulk. It's interior was divided into eight metal pens or cages, constructed on the middle deck with steel standards and woven wire. Each cage measured approximately forty feet by 20 feet and was 8 feet high. Into this small space there were fifty six beds, in which there were forty four men. The beds were stacked two deep, but, where one need only be four hours aboard a passenger boat, the men on the *Argenta* had to live there as a temporary home.

The deck was divided into eight compartments, by means of steel wire netting. The guards were a mixture of prison warders, 'B' Specials and regular British Army soldiers. A lot was written at the time of the conditions under which men were held on the ship. A massive human rights campaign highlighted the plight of the prisoners throughout Ireland, Great Britain and the U.S. To create living conditions for up to five hundred men on board a ship comparable to those provided for passengers travelling on third class was obviously inadequate for the needs of a growing prison population.

A correspondent wrote in the Freeman's Journal in June 1922:

> *The conditions under which 300 internees are imprisoned by the British Government on board the SS Argenta in Belfast Lough violate the elementary principles of health, impose slow torture on the prisoners, lend to the gradual undermining of their health and are so bad that, should any of the prisoners die as a result of them, it would be easy to frame the indictment for murder against those*

responsible for them.

Sir Dawson Bates under the Special Powers Act defended the conditions on board the prison hulk. In order to counter these allegations a delegation of English and American journalists was escorted around the prison to see for themselves, but the fundamental argument about the conditions continued for months. The prison population on board the hulk also continued to rise. These allegations of inhumane living conditions were vigorously disputed, however, by the Northern Ireland Government. The Government, to counter the allegations claimed that the conditions and space per prisoner on board the prison hulk were;

> *considerably in excess of that laid down by the Board of Trade for third class passengers. The bunks are the same for those provided for third class passengers and the whole upper deck is available for exercise. The fact that the top deck is surrounded by net wire seems to have given rise to a statement that the prisoners are kept in cages. As a matter of fact, the upper deck is so arranged and so extensive that games and tennis could be played.*

Nevertheless, letters continued to appear in the national press appealing to the Free State government to intervene.

> *The food with the exception of the bread, is of the worst possible description. badly cooked and served from the floor, there being no tables. The sanitary conditions are shocking. At each end of the deck on which the cages have been built are the latrines and urinals which are lying open. The pumping arrangements of the ship are not even capable of pumping a sufficient supply of water for the latrines which emit a most offensive odour permeating the entire deck. There is no hospital accommodation and no arrangements for isolating disease like the dreaded 'white scourge' (tuberculosis). One lifeboat was provided for evacuation in case of fire.*

By the end of July the prisoners had organised themselves to prevent individual prisoners from being isolated. Spokesmen were chosen to represent all the prisoners. A committee which had been formed to coordinate the internees in 'the Crum' was transferred *en masse* to the prison hulk in the Lough. The population on board continued to rise and the conditions subsequently became cramped. So cramped in fact that an outbreak of disease was feared as the temperature that summer continued to rise.

Headlines in the national press led with:

APPALLING CONDITIONS

... the worst feature of all is the living accommodation underneath, in which it is necessary to keep on the electric light all day. There are no tables from which the men can eat. They must use the soiled floor of their sleeping cages on which to cut up their food, which is served in bulk and in quantity and quality of the usual prison class. Fancy eating meat or margarine off a floor..?..for the latrines are closed after 8.00pm in the evening. The air is bad, the men sleeping two deep in an apartment, where the height from the floor to the ceiling is just 8 feet. In case of fire, which is very imminent on a wooden ship with palliasses (mattresses) filled with straw, there is only one lifeboat. Indeed the Craig Government do not appear to have made any provision for such an emergency.

On 22 August 1922, the *Argenta* was moved to Larne Harbour, in view of the approaching winter, where it was believed to have a safer shelter. On 14 September 1922, thirty six prisoners were removed to Derry jail because they had begun to organise protest action against their detention. Just prior to Christmas that same year two hundred prisoners who had gone on hunger strike were also moved to Derry jail. Due to the adverse publicity which the prison hulks received, the Northern authorities did their best to ensure that the *Argenta's* life was short. Some internees 'signed out' by promising to leave the jurisdiction of Northern Ireland. They were escorted to the border by the RUC. To those remaining however there seemed to be no respite in sight for their release from their incarceration on the ship. The civil war in the south ended with the 'cease fire' and 'dump arms' order of 24 May 1923, but prisoners were still held on the prison hulk. As a final attempt to gain their freedom the Bishop for Down and Connor, Joseph Mac Rory, attempted to intercede on their behalf. On 16 November 1923, he and thirteen others forwarded the following statement to Mr Baldwin, the British Prime Minister:

We the undersigned, representing the Catholics of the Six County area, beg to approach you in reference to the internees who have been held prisoners, many of them for close on two years, by the Northern Government.
They have now endured long and distressing confinement on board a convict ship and internment camp; and within the past sixteen days over one hundred and fifty were on hunger strike, many of them at the point of death, as a protest against their continued detention without charge or trial.
We ask how long are these conditions to be allowed to continue. Is it not time that the men should be tried and sentenced to punishment if found guilty, or released if nothing is found against them? They are all Catholics and the Catholics of this Northern area

*regard their detention in the circumstances one more proof of the
partisan and bigoted spirit of Sir James Craig's government.
Such a feeling on the part of the Catholics does not make for peace
in this area; and we put it to you that, in the interests of peace no
less than justice, all the internees should be released immediately
and without any of the degrading conditions that have been
pressed upon them hitherto.*

It was not until 1924 that the prisoners were released from the *Argenta* and Derry
jail. It is claimed that no one escaped from the ship because very few of its
prisoners could swim. One escape bid which had been recorded was that of Chuck
Brown. He succeeded in boring a hole through the side of the ship only to discover
that it was below the water line. His friends made him stand against the hole, his
body blocking the flow of water until help could be summoned.

The *SS Argenta* was used as an internment camp from 1922 until 1924. The ship
was eventually sold to a local businessman who broke it up for sale as souvenirs.
The Minister for Home Affairs, Sir Dawson Bates, bought the ship's brass bell for
fifteen shillings.

On the 22 December 1938, the Northern Ireland Government resorted to internment once again. Many men were arrested throughout the North. Three places of
detention were used: the prisons at Derry's Bishop Street and Belfast's Crumlin
Road and finally in October 1939, a prison ship called the *Al Rawadha*. This ship
was moored off the coast at Killyleagh in Strangford Lough, and visitors to the
prison had to come out in boats. The ship was only used for five months, but its
brief history is remembered vividly by those who were incarcerated there.

There was one abortive escape attempt from the ship. The prisoners were spotted
by one of the guards, who at first believed they were Germans. Forced to retreat
they knocked out one guard, and four of the five returned to their cells. One was
caught but afterwards released. One internee, Sean Gaffney, died while on the
boat. As a result of mounting pressure about deteriorating conditions on this prison
hulk the government finally moved to close it.

On 13 December 1971, internees were imprisoned on the government's new prison
in Belfast Lough—*HMS Maidstone*. The *Maidstone,* was built in 1937 and had
been used as an emergency billet for British troops in 1969. Soon afterwards it was
fitted out to be used as a detention centre for internees. The prison itself was
situated at the stern of the boat and consisted of two bunkhouses, one up and one
down, coupled with two mess rooms. Above these were the rooms of the Governor
and his staff and above this was the deck. The deck was surrounded with a ten foot

high barbed wire fence. Forward were the Army quarters, separated from the prison by a high mesh fence and a solid gate. The ship was moored at a jetty, twenty feet from the land, entry being guarded by sand bagged army emplacements.

On 16 February 1972, forty internees were transferred to Magilligan Camp, outside Derry. The transfers came one day before the ship's most notorious escape. 'The Magnificent Seven' have gone down in folklore as heroes in the republican communities from which they came. They managed to get through a port hole and swam ashore after reportedly monitoring the seals who used to breach the wire entanglements to approach the boat for food. Once ashore they commandeered a bus as far as the Markets area, from where they were soon spirited across the border. The Magnificent Seven were; Tommy 'Tucker' Kane, Tommy Gorman, Sean Convery, James Bryson, Peter Rogers, Martin Taylor and John 'Toddler' Toland. Almost as soon as they had reached dry land a ballad was being sung in Belfast pubs and clubs celebrating their daring escapade. *HMS Maidstone* was closed on 9 April 1972.

THE MAGNIFICENT SEVEN by Wolfhound

If you give me your attention it won't take very long
I'll tell you of a story that fills my heart with song
It's all about the *Maidstone* which is a prison ship
When seven of the prisoners gave the guards the slip.

It was on a Monday evening, when just to cause a lark
They said "Let's go and have a swim while it's nice and dark."
They swam across the water right to the other side
And the Belfast Corporation gave them a bus to ride.

They drove down to the Markets, which isn't very far
And there the local people, well you know what they are
They dressed them up in fine clothes, the colours they were gay
And before the Army could get there, the boys were far away.

Now the end of my great story, it is near at hand
Thank God all our swimmers, they are all on dry land
Their daring plan was brilliant I'm sure you will agree
"Success, success" it was the cry another seven free!

The door in Kilmainham Prison through which Simon Donnelly, Frank Teeling and Ernie O'Malley escaped in February 1921.

3. Inside Help

The Irish Republican Brotherhood (known as the Fenians) was founded by James Stephens on Saint Patrick's Day 1858. It was formed after the failure of the 1848 Young Ireland rising, in which many of the new organisation's members had taken part. The organisation grew in the Irish communities throughout the world, and reached such international proportions that it spread as far as America, Australia, New Zealand, and most parts of Northern Europe. The organisation infiltrated the British Army to such an extent that there were as many as eight thousand sworn members out of twenty-six thousand regular troops. It also spread its web to include members of the prison service. It was this type of infiltration which led to the successful escape of James Stephens just two weeks after he was captured in November 1865. The escape of James Stephens sent the Dublin Castle authorities reeling and was a major morale booster for the Fenian Movement, which had suffered many major set backs shortly before that.

The mass arrests of the Fenian Movement's most prominent members took place between September and November 1865. Leaders such as Jeremiah O'Donovan Rossa, John O'Leary, Thomas Clarke Luby, Charles J Kickham, Edmund Duffy and Hugh Brophy were all rounded up. Those arrested were charged with high treason and were held in Richmond Jail, off the South Circular Road in Dublin.

The man who was the leader of the Fenian Brotherhood throughout Ireland was James Stephens and the authorities were particularly delighted to have netted him in their catch. He was known as the Fenian Head Centre and all of Ireland was made aware of his capture. What the authorities had not planned for was the fact that no sooner was he in prison, than he would be back on the streets again. This was due to a dreadful miscalculation of trust coupled with Dublin Castle's inability to employ loyal warders.

Late on the night of 24 November 1865, and only two weeks after his arrest,

Stephens secured the necessary keys from the warders who were assigned to guard him. The only clue the other prisoners had to alert them that something had happened was the noise of frantic warders running from cell to cell in search of the government's most prized prisoner.

The two warders who were instrumental in his escape were John J Breslin and Denis Byrne, the night watchman, who was later arrested and charged with complicity. Stephens had, with their help, duplicated the keys. The conditions inside Richmond were somewhat different to the conditions which the political prisoners had previously encountered. In order to isolate the Fenians, all visits were forbidden. The portion of the jail selected for Stephens' confinement could not be approached without passing through a number of double-locked doors made of iron. Stephens was placed in cell number six in the cross range at the top of the prison, in a corridor which led to the eastern wing of the building. His cell was practically in the centre of the jail. Security at Richmond was extremely tight.

Stephens' cell door was composed of strong hammered iron and secured by a massive stock lock and a huge padlock. The corridor was also sealed with iron doors at each end, which were double locked. These were only the beginning of a series of security measures which Stephens had to overcome before reaching the outside. A large force of police was deployed to the jail and were posted to the surrounding streets. All communications addressed to the Fenian prisoners were opened and read before they were delivered, including those from friends and acquaintances. Every article of food and clothing, brought in was closely scrutinised, and every precaution was taken to prevent any opportunity of escape.

At 10.00pm on the night of Thursday 24 November, the warders made their last rounds of the cells. Stephens' cell door was checked. The keys had been handed over to the Governor earlier that evening at 5.00pm. The Governor had them deposited in their proper order in a special case in his office. Everything seemed to be safely under lock and key, as the saying goes, but nothing could have been further from the truth.

At 4.30am the night watchman, Denis Byrne, was doing his round when he discovered two tables stacked one on top of the other near the south western wall, adjoining the Governor's garden. Thinking that an escape was being attempted, he followed the security procedure and raised the alarm. There were no footprints on the soft ground by the table. The top of the wall, which was in a rotted state, was undisturbed. Obviously, the table had been placed by the wall, in an attempt to have the guards believe that this was how Stephens escaped, thereby covering up the collusion which existed between the warders and Stephens. The warders went into the prison to check that the Fenian prisoners were still in their cells.

When the Governor and his assistants rushed to the portion of Richmond Prison where Stephens was held, they saw the doors of the corridor and his cell lying wide open. The bed in which he slept was as it had been when last checked at 10.00pm. Books lay opened on a table as did several other personal belongings. The route through the prison was made without a single blunder, the only clue to the perpetrator's method being the duplicate master key, shining brightly and left deliberately in the last lock. In a feat of ingenuity which even the great Houdini would have found hard to accomplish, James Stephens had escaped from under their very noses.

What the Government had not accounted for was the Fenian movement's influence on the warders inside the jail. It soon became obvious that this was an inside job and so the hunt began to discover who aided Stephens' escape. It was blatantly obvious that the false keys would have been useless without an accomplice within the prison, as Stephens' cell door was doubly locked and could only have been opened from the outside.

The explanation of how the escape was accomplished came out years later. A wax impression was made by one of the warders, and was sent out to a local man to make a copy. Copies were also made of the master key which opened the gates through the corridors. Michael Breslin (brother of John Breslin of Catalpa fame) smuggled in the duplicate keys which had been made by Michael Lambert from the wax impressions. Stephens went to ground in Dublin and left for France in March of the following year. A huge reward was offered for his capture:

> *By the Lord Lieutenant-General and General Governor of Ireland*
> *A PROCLAMATION*
> *Whereas James Stephens has been an active member of a treason-able conspiracy against the Queen's authority in Ireland, and has this morning escaped from the Richmond Prison.*
> *Now we, being determined to bring the said James Stephens to justice, do hereby offer a Reward of*
> *ONE THOUSAND POUNDS*
> *to any person or persons who shall give such information as shall lead to the arrest of the said James Stephens and we do hereby offer a further Reward of*
> *THREE HUNDRED POUNDS*
> *to any person or persons who shall lead to the arrest of any one whomsoever who has knowingly harboured, or received, or con-cealed, or assisted or aided in any way whatsoever in his escape from arrest the said James Stephens.*

And we do also hereby offer a Free Pardon, in addition to the above-mentioned Reward, to any person or persons concerned in the escape of the said James Stephens who shall give such information as shall lead to his arrest, as aforesaid.

Given at Her Majesty's Castle of Dublin, this 24th day of November, 1865
By His Excellency's Command.

Following Stephens' escape from Richmond Bridewell, Kilmainham jail was turned into the top security prison where the Fenians would be held. Kilmainham had a long history of holding political prisoners, from the United Irishmen of 1798, Robert Emmet and those involved in that rebellion , the Young Irelanders of 1847, to the Invincibles of 1883. This jail had been opened in 1792. Kilmainham had been the scene of several escapes, the most notable being that of William Corbet and another man named Blackwell in December 1803. In the company of Napper Tandy, Corbet had been handed over to the English at Hamburg. Both men were officers in the French army under Napoleon and both were brought back to Ireland to stand trial. Corbet escaped and Tandy was finally released and allowed to return to France. In 1910 it had closed, but by 1914 it was being used by the British Army to accommodate troops at the outbreak of war. However in 1916 the jail was to be used once again to detain those involved in the uprising that Easter. After several weeks most of the prisoners were transferred to internment camps in England and Wales while the leaders were executed. Before long the place was empty, but the intensification of the War of Independence witnessed Kilmainham filling up once again with political prisoners.

Frank Teeling had been arrested after the IRA in Dublin took direct action against several members of the British Intelligence Service, in November 1920. Sentenced to death, he was held in a landing at Kilmainham known as 'Murderer's Gallery'. Teeling shared the landing with several other men who were also charged with murder, including Simon Donnelly and Paddy Moran. Another prominent leader who was present at the time was Ernie O'Malley. At the time of O'Malley's arrest and subsequent interrogation at Dublin Castle he was using the assumed name Stewart. It probably saved his life, for had the intelligence officers realised who he really was, he would most certainly have been killed. Frank Teeling had already been given a date for his execution, so plans to escape were hurried through and before long the prisoners had established a trusting cooperation with a British soldier who was stationed at the prison. Having made contact with the IRA on the outside, it was decided to smuggle in some guns and bolt cutters. The plan was quite simple and with the escort of the soldier through the prison the night of February 14th was chosen as the night to get away.

Like the Stephens escape, the whole affair would have been impossible without the inside help of someone who had access to all parts of the jail. Also, Kilmainham had not been used as a prison for some time and so there were sections of the jail which had not been refurbished with the proper deterrents to escape.

'Murderer's Gallery' was one such section. The guards here trusted that the sentries and constant patrols at strategic points throughout the prison would be enough to discourage any escape attempts. On this particular landing they simply bolted the cell doors without bothering with padlocks. The size of the spy holes in the doors meant that the prisoner could put his arm out and pull the bolt across. On the night in question, 14 February 1921, the prisoners simply pulled the bolt across and let themselves out of their cells. Having made their way along the corridor, they headed towards a door which had not been opened for many years. The doorway led directly onto a yard from which a gate opened onto a side street at the western side of the prison. The soldier who was helping them went down into this yard and with the bolt cutters opened the gate. The prisoners calmly walked out and with a nervous spring in their heels made off towards the city. Only three men went on the escape - Teeling, O'Malley and Donnelly. Paddy Moran, declined the opportunity to escape, believing he would have the charges against him dropped at his trial. Sadly he was proven wrong. He was taken out and executed the following month. Throughout the history of escapes many workers, warders and other members of staff have conspired with prisoners. Their collusion or suspected collusion has been the subject of inquiries and controversy right to the present day. One other similar event happened at Derry jail.

On 2 December 1921, an escape attempt which went drastically wrong ended with the death of two Police Constables named Lyttle and Gorman. As a result three men were sentenced to death. The Publicity Department of Dáil Éireann issued a statement, claiming that the circumstances of the escape and the death of the two policemen were being investigated by the Chief Liaison Officer. The Truce was still being negotiated between the British and Irish governments, and the representatives who were dealing with the British government wanted to show that they spoke with authority on behalf of all their people in Ireland:

> If the facts are as stated, and if enquiries prove that members of the
> IRA were implicated in an attempt to rescue the prisoners, this in
> itself constitutes a breach of discipline.
> Recently a general instruction was issued to all units of the Army
> that attempts to rescue prisoners constitutes a breach of the Truce.
> If this instruction has been infringed, severe disciplinary action
> will be taken against those responsible.
> Such tragic incidents as the deaths of Alderman Tadhg Barry in

*Ballykinlar Camp and Constables Gorman and Lyttle in Derry jail
are the direct consequences of the atmosphere engendered by the
prolonged imprisonment under conditions of exceptional hard-
ship during a Truce of thousands of men and women for their
political opinions. Incidents of this kind emphasise the fact that
these imprisonments constitute the greatest menace to the Truce.*

Menacing, the desire for freedom proved to be on that tragic night in December.
Inside the jail the prisoners with the help of one of the warders, Patrick Leonard,
overpowered the night guard. Outside the prison however the plan began to go
drastically wrong. Shortly after 2.00am two Special Constables named Reid and
Thompson spotted around a dozen men standing in the shadow of the prison wall
in Bennett Street. Just at that moment a rope was thrown from the inside of the
prison and was caught by one of those outside. The police opened fire on seeing
what they believed to be one of the prisoners on top of the wall. The shooting
startled the men in the street and they quickly made off with the Specials in pursuit.
The alarm was quickly raised and a search of both the immediate area around the
jail and also the prison itself was undertaken. Three cars were seized by the police
in Foyle Road. It was at this stage that the prisoners realised that the game was up
and their dreams of freedom had evaporated.

Inside the jail, as the military guard moved in they discovered the bodies of two
Special Constables lying just yards apart. Both men had been tied up and the
remains of cotton soaked with what was believed to have been chloroform lay
nearby. Two other warders were also found bound and gagged in the same corridor.
At the newly formed Stormont Parliament, the Northern Ireland Home Secretary,
Dawson Bates, was asked by the Unionist MP, Mr Coote to revise orders so that
there can be no possibility of having an "enemy within the prison" and to take such
steps as will ensure that the "prisoners are looked after by men who could be relied
on."

In response to these requests, the warders at Derry jail were replaced by members
of the Specials under the command of Captain Bass, the District Inspector from
Claudy. Three of the fifteen who were eventually charged with the double murder
were sentenced to death. They were; Temporary Warder Patrick Leonard, Thomas
McShea and Patrick Johnston. Three other prisoners, Patrick Tully, Henry Colgan
and Hugh Timmins were acquitted of the murder charge and were sentenced on
other charges. The court heard that the deaths of both policemen were due to
'asphyxia caused by chloroform and aggravated by a blow to the head.' All three
prisoners had their death sentences commuted to life imprisonment. They were
eventually released on 17 July 1926, and upon their release all three were served
with exclusion orders by the Northern Ireland Government.

Inside the jail, allegations of collaboration and collusion between warders and prisoners still remained the subject of rumour. For prison security advisers however such a situation was unforgivable. The prison system depends on the allegiance of its prison staff, and any flaw in that system could turn out to be a weakness which the prisoners would exploit. In today's top security prisons, even the movements of prison staff are severely restricted, thus keeping the chance of the successful manipulation of staff at a minimum. Nevertheless warders have been known to help in the conspiracies of political prisoners.

One of the biggest blows ever to prison service morale came with the discovery that one of their officers, who had access to the Emergency Control Room, admitted to conspiring with the IRA to help in a mass break-out from the Maze prison. It has always been a problem for the government. The escape committees always had the ability to penetrate prison security whereas the prison security chiefs have found it extremely difficult to find out what the escape committees' next move might be.

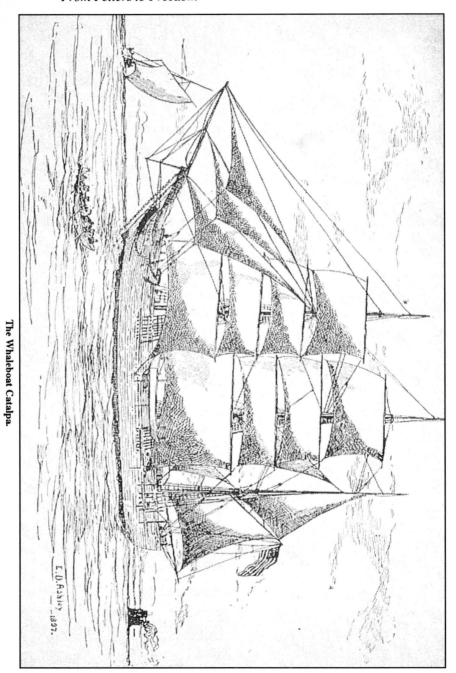

The Whaleboat Catalpa.

4. Marine Rescue.

> Oh, come all you gallant Irishmen and a story I'll relate
> I'll tell to you of the Fenian men who from the foe escaped
> Though bound with Saxon chains in a dark Australian Gaol
> They struck a blow for freedom, and for New York town set sail.

After the Fenian Rising of 1865-7 a lot of men were sent to the prisons in England. Sixty-three Fenian political prisoners were lined up along with three hundred and twenty criminal convicts at the harbour in Portland to board the *Hougoumont* to bring them to the Imperial Convict Establishment at Freemantle in Western Australia. Among them was a man named John Boyle O'Reilly. O'Reilly had been one of the soldier Fenians who had been transported to the colony for administering the Fenian oath to other British soldiers. It was claimed that O'Reilly wanted to take over the *Hougomont* en route to Australia, but the majority of other prisoners believed the risk to their lives was too great and so he abandoned his plans. Once they had arrived at the prison colony John Boyle O'Reilly began planning his escape. He had become very popular not only among the prisoners but among the local auhorities too. While working on the building of roads he had started a 'green party' and he was responsible for the saving of many old trees which had previously been earmarked for axing. Up until the 1950's there was a large old tree near Freemantle named 'O'Reilly's Tree'. While doing prison work he was constantly looking for opportunities to get away. Over the years he had built up a friendship with the warder's daughter and he eventually coaxed her to help him escape from the colony in August 1869.

The girl provided him with clothes and boots and, helped by three Englishmen, she arranged for him to board a boat at nightfall. The boat he had arranged to sail in had already left and so he eventually boarded an American whaling boat which unfortunately met with an accident and sank. He clung for his life to a plank for several hours before being rescued by a passing sailing boat. Soldiers who had, by this stage, realised that O'Reilly had escaped boarded the sailing boat but he was able to give them the slip. After throwing his hat into the sea they thought he had drowned. O'Reilly then made his way to Liverpool and from there to America where he became a celebrated newspaper publisher.

At the same time on the other side of the Atlantic a new movement was being established. That movement was called Clan na Gael. Many organisations were established among the Irish communities, especially after the exodus which followed the Famine and the 1848 Rebellion. Shortly after the Irish Republican Brotherhood was established in Ireland, the Fenian Brotherhood was founded in America. By 1866, that movement was split into two distinct factions, those who wished to channel all their resources to Ireland and those who wished to engage the British at Canada. By 1871, both factions were united again under the banner of Clan na Gael. It was several years before Clan na Gael and the IRB officially communicated with each other but when they did it was to be one of the most powerful organisations pushing for the establishment of a republic in Ireland.

In the following year there was a general amnesty and the majority of the political prisoners connected with the rising in Ireland were released. The terms of their release were that they must go into exile for the unexpired portion of their sentences. Many went off to America. One thing they brought with them was the desire to liberate the comrades whom they left behind in the convict settlement. Not all the political prisoners were released. Those who were classified as Fenian military prisoners were still held hostage by the government. These were the soldiers in British Regiments who were sworn members of the IRB.

At the annual convention at Baltimore of Clan na Gael the possible rescue of the Fenian military prisoners was first proposed. Extreme caution was necessary to avoid betrayal of the plot, but because such a rescue would have needed thousands of dollars to fund it, the planners had to put their ideas before committees in order to raise the necessary finance, thus exposing the rescue plans to a wide range of people. Having successfully lobbied some of the more influential delegates, Clan na Gael agreed to raise whatever funds were necessary to carry out the rescue. At the Baltimore Convention, a committee of ten men, whose job it was to see the rescue to fruition, was established. John Devoy was its chairman.

The first part of a three point plan was to buy a whaling vessel, select a suitable crew and sail to Australia. The second part was to send an organising party to Freemantle itself, disguised as either gold diggers or entrepreneurs. It would be their job to contact the six Fenian prisoners and ensure that they were on the beach to meet up with the landing craft which would take them out to the whaling boat. The final and most important part of the rescue was to land the rescued men at Fernandina,

Florida. This done they were to put to sea again to whale in the Atlantic in order to clear the expenses of the expedition.

John Boyle O'Reilly had made good his escape from the same prison colony on 18 February 1869, aided primarily by Captain Henry Hathaway of New Bedford. Hathaway had whaled the seven seas and it was said that he knew the Indian Ocean and the seas around Western Australia like no other. He gave a lot of advice to Devoy in the preparations for the rescue.

After a lot of shopping around, Devoy finally agreed to purchase a ninety foot whaler named *Catalpa* which he bought for $5,250. The next part of the plan was to select a suitable crew. The man chosen to lead the expedition was Captain George Anthony. It was left to him to select the rest of the crew. They would have to be a legitimate whaling crew so that no suspicion would be raised when they set out on their long voyage.

The *Catalpa* was moved from East Boston to New Bedford, where she was fitted out. The crew of the ship included only one Clan na Gael member, Denis Duggan. The rest comprised a proper whaling crew composed of men from the Malayan and Portuguese colonies of the Azores and Cape Verde Islands and Sandwich Island. The only people on board who had any inkling of the real purpose of the expedition, at that stage, were Captain Anthony and Denis Duggan.

J J Breslin was living in New York at the time of the rescue. He had been involved in the Stephens' escape from Dublin's Richmond Bridewell in 1865 and Devoy approached him to take part in the Freemantle mission. Devoy planned to send him to Freemantle to contact the prisoners. He was to be accompanied by Tom Desmond. Both men booked their passage on a steamer to Australia on 11 September 1875. Once they landed they soon made contact with a Fenian ex-prisoner named 'Ned' Kelly who in turn introduced them to two other IRB men named King and McInerney. Breslin and Desmond soon fitted in to the community and awaited the arrival of the *Catalpa*.

The *Catalpa*, did not set sail until May of the following year and did not reach Australia until 28 March 1876, having sailed east around the Cape of Good Hope and across the Indian Ocean. She finally dropped anchor at Bunbury Harbour, several miles from Freemantle.

Freemantle was built around the prison. The prisoners had only two places to go if they escaped, into the bush or out into the ocean. Both options were thought likely to fail because of the remoteness of the place and the danger of wild animals in the bush. Freemantle itself was a bustling town, nearly all of its inhabitants being convicts — or ticket-of-leave men as they were then called. These convicts all remained under prison discipline, and when the curfew bell rang at ten minutes to nine each evening they were obliged to be in their house for the night. This left the streets practically deserted. In the morning however the town was back to normal again.

Several prisoners however were not given the same amount of 'freedom' and it was amongst these men that the Fenian prisoners to be rescued were held. They were held inside the prison at Freemantle, but every day , because they were situated in such a remote place, the prisoners were detailed to various work gangs which went outside of the prison walls.

At the time of the rescue the Fenian prisoners had been in positions of trust in the jail and were engaged in a scheme several miles from the prison to construct a reservoir. An old Fenian and ticket-of-leave man named William Foley acted as envoy in and out of the prison to bring messages from Breslin to the men. Once the *Catalpa* had landed at Australia, the final plans for the rescue were conveyed to the Fenian prisoners. There were six in total; Martin Hogan, Thomas Darragh, Robert Cranston, Michael Harrington, Thomas Hassett and James Wilson.

Captain Anthony set off from Bunbury Harbour and dropped anchor about thirty miles off the coast at Freemantle. After selecting five of his best crewmen, he headed for the shore on Easter Monday, 17 April 1876. Breslin and Desmond were outside the gaol in the main street awaiting the emergence of the prisoners for their routine work detail. Both men drove a pony and trap, each vehicle containing a change of clothes ready for the escapees. The prisoners emerged in batches of three and at once jumped into the waiting carriages and headed to Rockingham beach, where the boat was waiting to take them out to sea.

As they arrived on the beach an onlooker, realising what was happening, immediately conveyed the alarm back to Freemantle, and the prison authorities set about their pursuit. Sixteen men were in the whaleboat and they had a considerable distance to go before they could board the *Catalpa*. The whaler was not noticed by the *Georgette* as it steered a path towards the *Catalpa*. They escapees watched disheartened, as the steamer pulled alongside. Before long they saw the *Georgette* pull away and return to Freemantle The First Mate, Smith, had refused to cooperate with the *Georgette*, whose crew, upon realising that the boat was flying the Stars and Stripes and was under the protection of the United States, returned to the colony for further orders. The whaleboat, on seeing the *Georgette* return to Freemantle, steered towards their landing craft. They were not out of danger yet. The Governor of Freemantle, enraged that six Fenian prisoners and their accomplices could have defied his authority, ordered the *Georgette* to take the *Catalpa* prisoner.

The prisoners had just boarded the *Catalpa* as the *Georgette*, flying a Man-o-War and Vice Admiral's flags, pulled up alongside yet again. This time, though, she was armed with a twelve-pounder field piece, an artillery unit and a detachment from the Water Police. They called on Captain Anthony to surrender the prisoners and fired a shot across her bow. Captain Anthony however maintained his stance and refused to cooperate, reminding the Captain of the *Georgette* that the *Catalpa* was in international waters and under the protection of the American flag. He was given fifteen minutes to reconsider his position but he refused to yield to their request. The *Georgette* took no further action and returned to Freemantle in the hope of seeking redress through governmental channels. The *Catalpa* meanwhile triumphantly bore a course towards the 'Land of the Free'.

A commission set up to investigate the escape slated not only the prison authorities but the local police force for their laxity in not noticing the suspicious behaviour of Breslin and Desmond. The Governor of the colony immediately set about introducing a campaign of reprisal. All the Fenian ticket of leave prisoners were returned behind bars. The work gangs were also returned to the gaol. This behaviour brought about a huge wave of disapproval from many sources as the age-old occupation of locking the stable door after the horse had bolted was brought into force. The local newspaper, *The Freemantle Herald* stated:

> *The general feeling was clearly one of pleasure that the pursuit had so far been unsuccessful. This arose chiefly out of the popular impression that the Fenian convicts are political prisoners, convicted and punished for offences against a government, not against society, and from the sympathy that the public everywhere display towards the weak in a contest against the strong.*

The police gave out the following description of the escapees:

> ***Thomas Darragh**, Imperial Convict Reg. No. 9707; arrived in the colony per convict ship Hougoumont, 10 January, 1868; Court martialled 2 March, 1866; charged with breach of the Articles of War. Sentenced to death, commuted to penal servitude for life. Description - Stout, age 42 years, height five feet six and a half inches, red hair, grey eyes, round visage, fresh complexion. Marks - Mole on right cheek; mole on breast; is much freckled; square shoulders, and walks erect. Fenian. Absconded from Freemantle 8.30am 17 April, 1876.*
> ***Martin Hogan**, Imperial Convict Reg. No. 9767; arrived in the colony per convict ship Hougoumont, 10 January, 1868; Court*

martialled on 21 August, 1866; charged with breach of Articles of War. Sentenced to penal servitude for life. Description - Stout, age 37 years, height five feet six inches, dark brown hair, dark hazel eyes, long visage, dark complexion. Marks - D left side; cut left eyebrow, walks firmly; has the gait and appearance of a cavalry soldier; is a coach painter. Fenian. Absconded from Freemantle 8.30am 17 April, 1876.

Michael Harrington, Imperial Convict Reg. No. 9757; arrived in the colony per convict ship Hougoumont, 10 January, 1868; Court martialled on July 7, 1866; charged with breach of Articles of War. Sentenced to penal servitude for life. Description - Middling stout, age 48 years, five feet seven and a half inches high, brown hair, grey eyes, full visage, sallow complexion. Marks - D left side; pockmarked. Fenian. Absconded from Freemantle 8.30am 17 April, 1876.

Thomas Hassett, Imperial Convict Reg. No. 9758; arrived in the colony per convict ship Hougoumont, 10 January, 1868; tried at court martial on 15 August, 1866; charged with breach of Articles of War and sentenced to penal servitude for life. Description - Middling stout, age 36 years, height five feet six inches, brown hair, light grey eyes, long visage, fresh complexion. Marks - D left side; cut mark left side upper lip; a rough carpenter. Fenian. Absconded from Freemantle 8.30am 17 April, 1876.

Robert Cranston, Imperial Convict Reg. No. 9702; arrived in the colony per convict ship Hougoumont, 10 January, 1868; tried at court martial 26 June, 1866; charged with breach of Articles of War and sentenced to penal servitude for life. Description - Middling stout, age 36 years, height five feet six and three-quarter inches, brown hair, grey eyes, oval visage, fresh complexion. Marks - Cross inside right arm, a farmer. Fenian. Absconded from Freemantle 8.30am 17 April, 1876.

James Wilson, Imperial Convict Reg. No. 9915; arrived in the colony per convict ship Hougoumont, 10 January, 1868; Court martialled on 20 August, 1866; charged with a breach of Articles of War and sentenced to penal servitude for life. Description - Middling stout, age 40 years, height five feet eight and a quarter inches, brown hair, grey eyes, oval visage, fresh complexion. Marks - D left side; is a labourer. Fenian. Absconded from Freemantle 8.30am 17 April, 1876.

Due to illness and the impatient desire by the escapees to land, the *Catalpa* finally docked in New York harbour to the great delight of its citizens. The Irish American press applauded the deed, and a reception was held for the men to celebrate their new-found freedom in the United States. When the *Catalpa* left to return to the Massachusetts port of New Bedford from which she had originally sailed, a welcoming party was assembled there. She was greeted by an artillery salute of seventy-one cannons, one for every state of the Union and one for every county in Ireland. The last shots they had heard were those of the British on board the *Georgette*. This time they were being hailed by the people in America as heroes. A public reception was held in Liberty Hall, in Dublin, where people scrambled to hear the true story of a truly remarkable episode in the history of the Irish peoples' continued attempts to be free.

Here's to the ship *Catalpa*, and the boys from Uncle Sam
And to all the Irishmen afloat and a Fenian to a man
Here's to Captain Anthony, bold Breslin and his crew,
When challenged by the Empire's might, the Stars and Stripes he flew.

The *Catalpa* expedition was the first of several marine rescue operations which have taken place during Ireland's prison history. Another took place at a prison colony in Cork Harbour known as Spike Island. This island, which is situated about a mile and half from the shore, was used as a monastic settlement in the seventh century. In the seventeenth century it was used to detain prisoners before they were transported as slaves to the West Indies. By 1790 it was being used as a fort and continued in that role until 1847 when the government found a use for it as a prison.

At around that time, the practice of transportation of convicted prisoners was coming under increasing pressure. The colonies to which the prisoners were usually sent became more and more reluctant to accept them, while at home pressure for the abandonment of this policy was growing. Faced with this situation the government began building their own prisons all over Ireland. Spike Island was one such establishment.

The basic task of the prisoners on the island, at least up until 1865, was to work on the fortifications. In the beginning, as many as two thousand prisoners were held on Spike Island in dank and wet barrack rooms. John Mitchel, the Young Ireland leader, was held there in 1858. By 1883 a reduction in the number of prisoners led to the closure of the prison and it once again reverted to a purely military use. By this time though, a huge amount of construction work had been completed on the island. In 1920 the place was soon opened up as a detention centre for internees and about five hundred men were housed there.

Two escapes were accomplished from this island prison in which ten men broke free. The first escape took place on 29 April 1921, and involved Sean McSwiney,

Con Twomey and Tom Malone.

As was stated earlier, the island was situated in Cork Harbour about one and a half miles from the shore. A moat surrounded the prison. Outside this moat was a golf course which was being constructed by prison labour. The island was constantly patrolled by a motor launch, and armed sentries kept watch for anyone approaching. By timing the motor launch and the routine of the sentries, an escape plan was soon hatched. It was estimated that the best time to carry out an escape was between 10.00am and 11.00am in the morning. The three men who planned to get out volunteered to work on the golf course. Their plan was to be rescued by boat and then transferred to a car on the mainland at the closest point to the island.

A motor launch with its Union Jack fluttering in the breeze set out from Cobh with four men on board. Heading for the prison island they could see the three men working at the shore at the preplanned point. Two guards were watching over them, one of whom was clearly armed with a rifle. Once the prisoners saw the boat out at sea they quickly attacked their guards and, confiscating the rifle and ammunition, they headed out towards the rescuing party. Once on board they sped towards the pick-up point on the shore. In the meantime the guards, who had been knocked out, awoke and raised the alarm. About two hundred yards from the shore the rescuing party could clearly see the military searching among the bushes on the island for their quarry, not realising that they had boarded the launch, which had previously appeared to be fishing off the coast. The three internees got clean away, as did those who volunteered to rescue them, both by boat and by car.

The second escape from the island needed a lot more detailed planning because improved fortifications of the prison—which included a series of moats, walls, sentries, searchlights and motorboat patrols—had to be breached. On 10 November 1921, the escape plan went into motion. Having worked on breaching the wall while on work-duty, seven prisoners with precise accuracy sneaked out past a patrolling guard on sentry duty and scaled the wall. This was the easiest part of the plan because after this the obstacle course was just beginning.

Beyond this wall, a forty foot wide moat had to be negotiated as had another wall, which was also patrolled by guards. Having successfully cleared this part of the course, they would then have to dodge searchlights to make it to the edge of the island which was still a half mile from land. At 5.00pm, having safely bluffed the count, all seven went off. The seven were; Moss Twomey, Bill Quirke, Tom Crofts, Dick Barrett, Henry O'Mahony, Patrick Buckley and Jack Eddy. Clearing the obstacles with the agility of cats, they made their getaway in a boat which had been moored at the pier of the island that night, and under the cover of darkness they rowed towards dry land and freedom.

Another marine rescue which would carve a place in the story of prison escapes was that planned by the GHQ of the IRA in 1924. This involved the use of the Republican motor launch, the *St. George*. A communiqué was sent to the IRA from the internees at Larne internment camp from where the prisoners had planned a mass escape, which would involve about fifty men getting out. The plan was to tunnel out of the camp and to be rescued from the shore by a boat which would then drop the men further down shore where they could be transferred to safety.

Sean McBride was picked to lead the rescue mission. He chose three of his best soldiers, Tom Heavey, Tony Woods and Frank Barry, to crew the rescue vessel. McBride was also given the job of choosing a suitable boat for the rescue mission. He finally purchased an eighty foot, cruising vessel through the Belfast shipyard of Workman and Clarke & Co. Ltd for £200. The craft had been built in Canada as a submarine chaser but by the time McBride bought it, it had been converted for use as a cruising vessel by the linen merchants, Lindsay of Belfast. Before she could be used, the engines of the sixty ton boat had to be overhauled. This work was completed by McBride and his three crewmen at Workman Clarke's yard at Belfast, seventeen miles from Larne.

In the meantime the internees were burrowing their way out as all the strands of the escape plan began to come together. Then on 13 December, the day before the proposed rescue, McBride received a communiqué from the prisoners indicating that the tunnel had been discovered. After confirming the communiqué's authenticity, the *St. George* left Belfast on course for Southampton. Sailing down the coast, the boat developed engine trouble at Dundrum Bay. A storm arose in the middle of this difficulty and the crew of the Republican motor launch had to be rescued by the coast guard.

The Larne tunnellers did not have to wait long before they tasted freedom once again however. All the internees were released from the camp on Christmas Eve 1924.

Mountjoy Prison from the banks of the Royal Canal, Dublin.

5. Get us in to get you out.

At times in the escapologists' history, the introduction of a rescue team appeared to be the only way of getting people out of the prison. As time went on the risks involved in this sort of escape meant that many schemes did not go ahead and other methods of escape had to be explored. During the time of the Fenian Movement's activities in Britain, several such rescues were, accomplished. One original method of escape was to break into the jail to effect a rescue, instead of leaving it to the limited resources of the prisoner to break out. This was, most times, achieved by various methods of disguise to gain entrance to the jail in question. It has been used to successful effect on many occasions, most notably in 1925 at Mountjoy Prison.

One of the first times this method was implemented was at Cork Jail on 11 November 1918. At that time Donnachadh McNeilus, a Donegal man, was being held at the prison. Six armed volunteers entered the jail on the pretext of visiting the prisoner, after it was learned that McNeilus and other untried prisoners were allowed one ten-minute visit from two visitors each day.

All six volunteers duly gained access to the prison on the pretext of visiting different prisoners. Outside the jail other volunteers took up their positions. The telephone wires were cut. Those who were visiting McNeilus were Joe Murphy and Martin Donovan. Once they were inside, a warder came to escort them to the visiting cell. At that moment a party of British soldiers also came to the door. Upon knocking and gaining entrance, they proceeded into the prison grounds. McNeilus' visitors made to get up, indicating that their visit was finished. As they did so the warder placed the key in the lock to let them out. At that precise moment Murphy and Donovan were upon him and, while they were relieving him of his keys, McNeilus jumped over the barrier and ran off through the gate and into the prison grounds, quickly followed by his two companions. Meanwhile in the waiting room, the other four volunteers had been sitting for several minutes while Murphy and Donovan were taken to the visiting cell. They overpowered the warder in this section of the jail and disconnected the telephone. After tying him securely, they then opened the gates leading to the visiting cell as McNeilus and the two other men in the rescue party arrived. Locking all the gates behind them as they went they let themselves out of the jail without a hitch. Once outside the jail and not being fully briefed of the prison escape McNeilus jumped onto another volunteer's bicycle and pedalled away. It was several hours before the rescue party caught up with him again to bring him to safety.

This procedure was used by Michael Collins shortly before the Truce when he, along with 'The Squad', decided to free Sean McEoin from the clutches of the hangman. McEoin who had been the leader of a Flying Column in County Longford who was captured after an ambush and had been sentenced to death. He was due to face the hangman after a court-martial was held in Dublin on 14 June 1921. The IRA, aware of McEoin's fate, decided to rescue him and made elaborate plans to ensure that he was at the Prison Governor's office when they gained entry to the jail complex. Intelligence reports indicated that if the guards were presented with a Prison Removal Order the rescue party would be safely let in through the main gates and allowed to proceed unhindered to the Governor's office.

'The Squad' was a new and formidable IRA unit formed in September 1919. This unit was unique simply because their intelligence network was second to none. It was principally due to this outstanding attribute that they were given the job of rescuing McEoin from Mountjoy Prison shortly after his committal to that jail. To achieve their goal, Collins made contact with a warder who was prepared to do some work for them. This warder worked at Mountjoy Prison and he furnished the squad with details on staffing, times and other relevant details. A message was sent in to McEoin that he was going to be rescued and that he had to make sure he was in the Governor's office the following morning from 10.00am.

Meanwhile the other members of 'The Squad' had been watching the movements of an armoured car at the Dublin Abattoir. It was their intention to drive in to the jail with this vehicle, but first of all they had to capture it from the soldiers who were driving it. Every day this carload of soldiers accompanied lorries to the abattoir to collect rations for several barracks in and around the city. They noticed that the soldiers usually got out of the vehicle to stretch their legs (against all orders, of course). This breech of security was all the IRA needed to enable them to gain control, and before long a Rolls Single Turret Whippet became the property of the IRA in Dublin. Unfortunately it was not captured on the morning that was initially planned and McEoin was standing in the Governor's office talking for as long as he could before finally being brought back to his cell in 'C' Wing. A message was brought in telling him to be at the Governor's office the following morning at the same time.

Joe Leonard and Emmet Dalton were waiting at a prearranged pick up point for the Whippet. Both were dressed in British Army uniforms and both were armed. The time was 10.00am. Pretty soon they were on board the vehicle and heading for the gates of 'The Joy.' Producing the Prisoners Removal Order to the sentry at the outer gate, they found themselves in the courtyard. The gate was slammed shut behind them. There were another two gates before them and these were opened also. Emmett Dalton and Joe Leonard proceeded unhindered right up and in to the Governor's office. When they entered they were surprised to find the Governor and seven of his staff there. Overnight a new batch of soldiers had been garrisoned at the jail and on that particular morning they were being introduced to all of the prisoners individually so as to be acquainted with them. All the normal day to day procedures at the jail, were cancelled for that day and McEoin had been told at 9.30am that he would not be allowed to see the Governor until the afternoon.

Inside the office the Governor still did not know the real purpose of the soldiers' visit. Once he claimed that he would have to check with the Dublin Castle authorities, the two IRA men had no choice but to draw their guns and take everyone in the room prisoner. When they had them all safely tied up they both headed back out the way they came.

Outside the prison another IRA team rushed the front gate. In the process a soldier, noticing what was happening opened fire. The IRA team commenced firing at the sentry and killed him just as Dalton and Leonard came rushing out of the prison. Realising their rescue had not gone according to plan they continued with their plans of securing a safe passage out of the jail in the armoured Whippet, the British Army firing after them. They burned the Whippet at Marino and everyone dispersed. Sean McEoin was released in August 1921, as part of the Truce negotiations and was later elected as a TD to Dáil Éireann.

When the Truce and eventually the Treaty were signed, Mountjoy Prison became the centre of some harrowing tales of prison life. During the Civil War the jail was used by pro-treaty forces to imprison those republicans who were then known as anti-treaty. A bitter battle was fought between both sides as the eyes of the world watched to see if there was finally going to be a settlement to the Anglo-Irish conflict. Meanwhile the prisons began to fill up once more. Several tunnels were dug from outside the jail but when these were discovered an unsuccessful attempt was made to overpower the guards. This resulted in four deaths.

The most effective prison rescue took place at Mountjoy Prison in 1925. On a cold Dublin winter evening in November, nineteen prisoners escaped after the prison staff were held up inside the jail. The plan for this escape was inspired at an IRA Convention which was held in Dalkey on 14 November 1925. The scheme was to bring two 'poachers' to the prison in the company of 'the police' with warrants duly signed for their committal. These prisoners had to be from an area more than twenty-five miles from Dublin, otherwise they would be automatically committed to the Bridewell.

When the plans were finalised and the prisoners acquainted with the scheme, three poachers in the company of three policemen, one of whom (George Gilmore) was a Sergeant, drove up to the outer gate. Telling the guard that the prisoners were to be taken in to serve three months, *in lieu* of paying their fines, they were allowed to enter through the main gates as far as the second gate. At this point Gilmore got out of the car and produced a revolver which he stuck into the back of the unsuspecting warder, taking his keys. To enter the main prison they had to pass through another gate which was guarded by armed Free State soldiers. With unconcerned coolness Gilmore approached the armed sentry and asked for a light. The soldier, not knowing his predicament, set down his rifle to do the favour and found himself taken prisoner also.

Securing control of both gates the rescuing party now had full access to the prison. With their inside knowledge of the jail they proceeded, taking hostages of whatever warders they met as they approached 'the circle', which was where the four wings met. Here was their final gate. Gilmore gave the shout, "Three on!" and the warder on the other side simply let them in. Nineteen men escaped including Jim Colin, Mike Carolan, Sean Russell and Dave Fitzgerald. Once the prisoners made their way to freedom they found, to their great dismay, that there was only one car waiting to pick them up, and so the mad scramble to evade capture began on foot.

6. Prison Files.

Jails up until quite recently were basic affairs. The usual three landings in the building were lined each side with a series of cells. Bars on the windows, set in concrete, were all that divided the prisoner from the outside world. As the jails further developed, a twenty foot high wall was built around them. This was the only obstacle which prisoners had to overcome on most occasions. Once they escaped the prisoners had to put a good distance between themselves and the jail. This was, in most instances, not possible without outside help, both for the smuggling of the hacksaw blade and helping in the getaway.

During the night of 18 October 1922, the quiet population of Sligo were awakened by gunfire. Some time after 2.00am the courthouse came under attack from various points, the object being to engage the military and thus cover up the coup which was in progress at the jail. There are a number of stories told as to how the prisoners managed to get away, but the escapees appear to have carefully planned and arranged the escape. The bars of certain cell windows had been filed through, and when the time came, they were quickly removed by the prisoners. Sheets were used for ropes where no rope was available and the outer walls were scaled by some means, as yet not clear.

As soon as it was discovered that the prisoners had escaped the troops took up positions at various roads leading out of the town. Three men were recaptured immediately. Some who had escaped had just been arrested the previous Sunday and others had been arrested at Tubbercurry a fortnight before. Over fifty prisoners had been removed from Sligo Jail to Longford, and therefore, an even greater escape was avoided. Many other prisoners were to escape in a similar manner, but all had one thing in common — each one filed through the bars on their cells.

In February 1966, Ireland was preparing for a series of commemorations for the fiftieth anniversary of the Easter Rising. The previous year Princess Margaret had visited Ireland and stayed at Abbeyleix, County Laois. Trees were felled, bombs went off and ten men were eventually brought before Limerick Court. The arrests sparked serious protests in that town. Later in the year, a British Army gunship made a courtesy call at Waterford, shots were fired at her and three men were sentenced for possession of an anti-tank gun. The three were the only political prisoners held in Limerick Jail at the time. Again a lapse in security was exploited to the full, and as a result, one of the three, Richard Behal got away. All three men were regularly moved about inside the jail and at the time of the actual breakout they were put into cells on the upper landing. The day picked to go out coincided with the twenty-first birthday of the daughter of the prison Governor, Denis O'Donoghue. A party was being held at the Governor's residence which was inside the prison grounds. The escape was only discovered the following morning when the warders unlocked the cells. The bars in Behal's cell had been sawn through and the prisoner and the bedclothes were missing. The warders immediately ran out onto the landing and set off the alarm. It was too late however Behal was already long gone. It later transpired that a team broke into the prison grounds to help him escape. In his home town of Kilkenny, the usual rapturous reception had to be curtailed, as Behal went to ground. Several weeks later he made an impromptu appearance at a local parish hall, where he gave a speech to a captivated audience.

The hacksaw blade came to be the most essential tool of all escapers. Prison bars were usually the only obstacle to the potential escapee and the only tool which could get through them would be the hacksaw. Some have sawn through the bars in less than a week, others have taken far longer. Regular searches by the warders meant that the escapee had to work as quickly and as quietly as possible. As was the case in Limerick Jail, prisoners were not kept for any length of time in the same cell, thereby making the preparation for an escape more difficult.

The first man to saw the bars at Belfast Prison was James McCann. 'The troubles' were getting increasingly worse by the day and Belfast Prison was getting prepared for another influx, as usual. Martin Meehan was one of those who ended up inside the jail in those early days after being charged with having a gun at the funeral of Barney Watt. He was placed on remand at 'C' Wing. Before long he had the company of James McCann. McCann had been arrested with two other anarchists outside Queens University Common Rooms. The three had been charged with possession of petrol bombs and a shotgun. When the RUC approached the three, James McCann produced the shotgun. After a brief struggle they were subsequently arrested and put on remand.

Martin Meehan takes up the story:

"This particular man, McCann, was something that I had never experienced before

- he was a character of characters and he happened to be put into the same cell as me. He kept on saying, 'this place isn't big enough to hold me. I'm going to break out of here.' Well I thought that he was just talking off the top of his head, until, one day he came back from a visit with two hacksaw blades down the legs of his trousers. He had noticed that in the mornings, visits were highly disorganised and the screw who should have been watching the visit from up in an observation box was always missing from his post. He had arranged to have his visit early in the morning, taking advantage of the disorganisation. There were wire grilles at that particular stage on remand which divided the prisoner from his visitor. Nevertheless his visitor was able to push the blades through the wire mesh without being seen.

"The two of us decided to go out. At that time there was no real structure in the jail with only seven or eight republicans as such. These included men like Billy McKee, Frank Card, John Joe Magee and Paddy O'Hara. Anyway, McCann brought back two blades and the two of us actually sawed the bars for about three weeks. We were almost through when the screws started to put grilles on the outside of the cell widows at 'C' Wing as added security. We knew that we would not have got through the bars by the time they reached our cell window. The scaffold was moved along to our cell and we realised our luck was in.

"What happened was, there was this trade screw who was say sixteen or seventeen stone and he never got up on the scaffold, instead he got the prisoners to do it. As luck would have it two of the prisoners were well known to me. They were from Clonard and Ballymurphy. So the screw sent these two up to put the bars on and tighten the bolts. They worked right through dinner hour and we were locked up during this time. We didn't have any actual contact with them as they were sentenced prisoners and we were on remand.

"That particular dinner time they were putting the outer bars on our cell. I was inside the cell at the time and the prisoners thought I was messing about. They had the scaffold right up to the window. I said 'I'm not winding you up, I'm deadly serious.' 'Ach give my head pace' he says. 'I know your crack, it's only a wind up.' We had butter round the bars where they were cut and I rubbed the butter away and showed him the cuts on the bars on the inside of the window. He agreed to only tighten one side of the bars and leave the other side hand-tight. The scaffold was then taken down and moved along to the next cell windows. As far as we were concerned we were going ahead with the plan. On the day before we were to go, Billy McKee came to me and advised me against escaping telling me that I was probably going to beat the charge I had against me. Anyhow I got moved and the next day McCann went out.

"He had made rungs and a hook out of chair legs and he also had made a rope with sheets knotted together. At about 7.00am he made his move, timing it between the change of the guards. There were soldiers in the pill boxes but McCann had it all timed to precision. He had been watching their every move. He dropped down into 'C' Wing yard and got up onto the shed. He scrambled over the wall, down into the wood yard, and over to the gate. He then put all the rungs he had made from chair legs into the gate to make a makeshift ladder and climbed up them. This particular gate didn't go to the top of the wall - he had another fifteen feet to go. He held on with one hand at the top of the gate and he threw the hook up and then when it caught he pulled himself up. He then walked along the wall towards St Malachy's College and got away.

"I had given him the address of a mate in the New Lodge and he arrived there at about 7.40am just as the fella was going to work. He said to him, 'Martin Meehan sent me down.' Because of his accent, which was not your usual Belfast brogue, the fella was taken aback. He was suspicious of him but no sooner had McCann spoken when the siren went off in 'the Crum'. He was brought into the house, cleaned him up and escorted over the border. I eventually met up with him again in the Free State about Christmas 1971."

The previous escape from 'the Crum' was similar to that enacted by McCann. On Boxing Day 1960, twenty one year-old Daniel Donnelly from Omagh and John Kelly from Adela Street, Belfast, sawed through the bars of their cells. New alterations at the jail had been undertaken to hinder any repeats of past security breakdowns. The walls had been built higher and searchlights and watchtowers had now been installed. Both men were undeterred by these new security measures and after careful timing they climbed down into the prison yard. What up to then had been an escape operation with no hitches, then began to go drastically wrong.

Both men had been held at 'A' Wing of the jail, directly behind the warders' houses, which face onto the Crumlin Road. This wing is where all the long-term political prisoners were held. At the time Donnelly had been studying for a degree while serving ten years for causing an explosion while Kelly had been serving an eight year sentence for possession of guns and ammunition. Three bars in the cell window had previously been filed through in Kelly's cell. After evening meal, the usual regime was that the prisoners were allowed out of their cells for a period of free association. It was at this stage that Donnelly entered Kelly's cell. The three bars were removed and both men lowered themselves into the yard with a seventy foot rope which they had made from strips of sheets, blankets and electrical flex knotted together.

They successfully avoided the probing searchlights and arc lamps and made their way across the yard to the wall behind the warder's houses. They then threw the rope up and secured it to the top of the wall by means of a hook. Dan Donnelly went up and over the wall first. He dropped down the other side into a passageway behind the houses. Kelly meantime made his way up the rope. Just as he reached the top the rope suddenly snapped and Kelly came hurtling down to the ground with a thump. Donnelly quickly realised that something had happened to Kelly at the other side of the wall and made his way out onto the main Crumlin Road through a gate near the Masonic Hall. Kelly was discovered several minutes later by a patrol of warders who immediately raised the alarm. Once the alarm went off the prisoners inside the jail were counted and after the warders had ascertained that an escape was afoot they set off the prison siren as messages were sent to police stations to raise the alert.

Within four minutes of the escape the roads surrounding the prison were sealed off. The passengers on the Heysham boat were checked and all those people at the airport were scrutinised. Cross border roads were also patrolled by RUC and 'B' Specials in a vain attempt to catch Donnelly, but to no avail. He had been picked up on the Crumlin Road still attired in his grey prison uniform with the red star on the arm. He changed clothes in the car and was brought to safety. After a fortnight he turned up in Monaghan.

The local papers reported how people in the east of the city first became aware that something had happened when they heard three loud explosions accompanied by the launch of bright flares from the new police headquarters at Castlereagh. This had been the first time that such a signal had been used and many of the residents in that area were concerned that the station itself was under attack. The radio news soon informed them of the escape as the search for Donnelly continued.

The reliant hacksaw blade which they used was never found. Security bosses immediately sat down to plan tighter measures at all the jails not only throughout the UK, but throughout Ireland also. Their theories of prison management were still on the drawing board when the Civil Rights marches in the 1960's prompted calls for internment and imprisonment once again.

The Alouette helicopter which was used to free three members of the IRA from Mountjoy Prison on 31 October 1973.

7. The Joy of Freedom.

Mountjoy Jail was built as part of the relief work of the 'Famine' period. It is the newest prison in Dublin and in 1919 held many political prisoners. One of these men was Robert Barton. Barton had been an important leader in the Republican Movement at the time, and was later part of the team which went to London to negotiate the Treaty. In March of that year a protest against the criminalisation of republican prisoners in Mountjoy was deliberately curtailed in order to lull the prison authorities into a false sense of security. During several different protests at the jail concerning the treatment of sick prisoners Barton found himself removed to a ground floor cell. All that remained for him to do was to saw through the bars on his cell window. With the help of republicans on the outside, a file was smuggled in and in just three days he had successfully cut one of the bars. On 16 March, Barton made his escape after rigging up a dummy which he placed under blankets in his bed in order to fool the watching guards. The warders checked each individual cell with a cursory glance through the spy hole in the door and Barton's dummy passed for a sleeping prisoner. Barton meanwhile, had climbed out of his window into the yard and quickly scaled the wall. He accomplished this after he threw a piece of soap over to a prearranged spot, as a form of signal. Volunteers threw back a weight to which a rope was attached. He climbed to the top of the wall and jumped into a blanket which broke his fall at the other side. He was then spirited away to a safe house in the Donnybrook area.

On 29 March 1919, only thirteen days after Barton's successful breakout yet another embarrassing flaw in prison security was spotted and availed off to the utmost success. On this occasion twelve prisoners were to escape, among them Padraic Fleming and the four prisoners who had to curtail their protest and thereby lulled their guards into a false sense of security. The subsequent security lapse was taken advantage of much to the embarrassment of the authorities in Mountjoy. On 29 March the prisoners were brought out for their usual exercise. There were three distinct groups, J J Walsh and Piarais Béaslaí, who exercised in front of the hospital wing, Padraic Fleming and the bulk of the political prisoners who exercised in a field just inside the wall and the four prisoners around whom the protest had originally centred. They were still being punished for their previous actions and as such exercised in a cage in the yard which was always guarded by a large group of prison warders. The prisoners came out at 2.30pm. The escape was set for 3.00pm. The signal came from outside the wall in the form of a shrill blast on a whistle. The prisoners immediately ran to the wall at the rear of the hospital. The men in the cage rushed their guards and were quickly alongside their comrades. Fortunately on that particular day the number of warders guarding them had been drastically reduced, making their assignment relatively easy to accomplish. Those who had been chosen to act as a rearguard held up all the unarmed warders by pretending that they had guns hidden in their pockets. The warders, thinking better of it, obeyed their orders and offered no resistance whatsoever. A weight with a rope attached then came over the wall and in time-honoured fashion the traditional rope ladder appeared and the scramble to freedom was repeating itself all over again.

Everyone who escaped on that occasion got away safely on bicycles and trams. The breakout was hailed as an amazing success, even by the authorities, considering that it took place in broad daylight and not one person was captured or injured.

> The first was bold Barton - when he was departin'
> Left a note for the boss - his politeness to show
> And a dummy in order - to fool the poor warder
> But Barton has popped it - Alive , alive oh
>
> J J Walsh and Pearce Beaslai - the trick did quite easily
> Some pro-German devils - a ladder did throw
> Then some twenty Sinn Féiners - like acrobat trainers
> Scaled the wall to their freedom - Alive , alive oh

Alive, alive oh. Alive, alive oh. Sinn Féiners and pro-Germans, alive, alive oh! (Popular Dublin ballad to the tune of Molly Malone)

Two other major escapes were to take place at Mountjoy in the 1920s. One was of four republican women at the jail on 30 October 1920 and the next involved seven men who also successfully outwitted their guards at the end of November 1921. All seven had been convicted by military courts and were held in 'the Joy'. At 5.30pm when daylight was fading, the seven, Thomas Keegan, William Troy, Patrick O'Brien and Leo Fitzgerald from Dublin, Gerald Dixon from Athlone along with Sean Keating and Patrick Rigney from Cork, all left their cells. Previous to this the prisoners had acquired a revolver and ammunition which they kept

concealed within the prison. It was Armistice Day and the usual detachment of
Auxiliaries at the prison had gone to a social engagement in dress suits. They
foolishly left their uniforms unprotected in a section of the prison to which
Republican prisoners had access. When the time came the prisoners dressed in
military uniforms overpowered the warder on the landing and having secured the
keys, quickly let themselves through the internal doors.

They then sauntered up to two warders who were guarding the main gate. These
two asked for identification and in the process they too found themselves as
prisoners of the escaping party. The door keys were secured here and the gates
opened. Shots were fired at the escapees from a Lewis gun which was mounted in
a sentry post overlooking the front of the jail but no one was hit. The official
statement, issued from Dublin Castle was brief and to the point. It declared:

> *Between 5 and 6 o'clock last night seven male prisoners made their*
> *escape. Inquiries are in progress.*

In the aftermath of the Four Courts Battle in July 1922 all the civilian prisoners were
moved from the Male Prison, Mountjoy, and this part of the jail was converted into
a solely Military Prison. In October 1922, Peadar Breslin and three prison guards
were shot dead during a botched escape attempt. As a result of this, many more
stringent security measures were imposed by the jail authorities.

In November 1925, a cold Dublin winter evening was interrupted by another daring
escape from the confines of 'The Joy'. On that occasion nineteen prisoners escaped
after the prison staff were held up inside the jail when a rescue team entered the
prison with forged warrant papers.

This escape was followed by many attempted escapes the most notable on 11
October 1931. On that occasion George and Charles Gilmore, who had both been
arrested and held at 'the Joy' in connection with an arms find earlier in the year, tried
to get away. As the men overpowered the warder guarding them in the prison yard,
a rescue team were taking control of a house at Glengarrif Parade. This row of
houses backed on to the prison yard and the plan was to simply throw a rope over
from the yard of the house at the appropriate time. The Gilmores could then scale
the prison wall, go out through the front door into a waiting car and make good their
escape. At the prearranged time, George Gilmore grabbed the warder and held him
up using an imitation gun. He then took the warder's keys and threw them over the
wall into the yard of the house as a signal for the rope to be thrown over. Nothing
happened however and after about fifteen minutes the two Gilmores were overpowered. The police and military meanwhile pulled up outside the front door of the
house at Glengarrif Parade where the keys were thrown.

The occupants claimed that four men had just left. They had taken over the house twenty minutes earlier and had instructed the family to stay in the front room, telling them that everything would be over in a short while after which they could contact the police. The police recovered a rope ladder with steps and two six foot ladders. The prison was used again when internment was introduced during the Second World War but at that time was noted more for the executions which took place there rather than the scene of escapes or escape attempts.

During the Border Campaign 'the Joy' was once again used to house political prisoners. This time only twenty two were held at 'D' Wing of the prison. On Sunday 13 April 1958 the guard decided to conduct a headcount. His count resulted in a search as sixteen men were unaccounted for. All of the men were discovered in a basement cell about to go out through a tunnel which they had been constructing for some time. It was believed that the plan was to tunnel from the cell to the courtyard, which was still within the prison grounds. From here they would have been assisted from outside to scale the perimeter wall which runs along the Royal Canal at the rear of the jail. On 7 May another attempt by the prisoners to breakout ended in a fistfight in the yard adjacent to the same wall. As a result of all the attempts the prisoners were eventually transferred to the Curragh. The Curragh was no different from Mountjoy and before long several escapes took place from that camp also.

With the escalation of violence in the North in the early 1970's Mountjoy was used once again to hold Republicans, and by this time, Loyalist prisoners. From past experience the prison authorities knew to be on alert for possible escape attempts. After all, most of the advisors up until that point had been in camps and jails themselves during the War of Independance. They knew what sign to look out for and by July 1973 had avoided any embarrassing breaches of security and had settled down in the misguided belief that they knew how to hold their prisoners securely. That month they almost intercepted a rescue team who had thrown one hundred feet nylon ropes over the prison wall, after securing an end to the windows of a derelict house adjoining the jail. A subsequent search of the house by Gardaí uncovered signalling equipment, which, it was believed would have been used that night to give the 'all clear' sign. The warders in the Joy were therefore on the alert that something might take place. What happened next took them completely by surprise.

By far the most spectacular escape ever recorded in Ireland took place at the jail on 31 October 1973. In scenes which had only been recorded on the set of a James Bond movie, a hijacked helicopter landed in the exercise yard in the middle of the afternoon and whisked three of the IRA's leading activists to freedom. Seamus Twomey, Chief of Staff of the Provisionals, J B O'Hagan, who was allegedly the

IRA's quartermaster and Kevin Mallon, who had been in jail in the 50's for IRA activity along the border, were the three men chosen to go. The men's daring rescue was followed by cheers and applause from the other prisoners in the yard while the warders stood mesmerised unable to prevent their escape.

On 21 August the Receptionist at Irish Helicopters at Westpoint Hangar, Dublin Airport, had received a booking from a man with an American accent to hire a helicopter for some film location shooting in County Laois. The day previous to the incident (30 October 1973) the 'film maker', Mr Leonard, arrived at the heliport to view the helicopter for its suitability. He eventually chose an Alouette II because of its seating capacity for five persons. The following day at around midday Mr Leonard arrived once again and this time they went off to view the film site from the air. The helicopter and its two passengers touched down at a field at Stradbally around two hours later. Upon landing, the unsuspecting pilot saw two men coming out from the trees before him. He was then told of the IRA plot and immediately received his new orders. Mr Leonard went off into the trees with one of the IRA men and the captain of the helicopter took off again with the remaining man, armed with an armalite rifle keeping him under a close watch. Captain Thompson Boyes was forced at gunpoint to fly to Mountjoy following the path of the Royal Canal and railway lines. They flew at a height of one thousand feet. He was not allowed to contact Air Traffic Control to register his flight path and he became worried in case he crashed into any civilian aircraft. As he entered the Dublin area he dropped the helicopter to a height of seven or eight hundred feet and approached the prison from the rear. The helicopter touched down in the centre of the compound outside D Wing where the political prisoners had been out for exercise. It was a hazardous landing as the blades had only a twenty foot clearance to the walls on every side. The pilot tried to explain that the Alouette may not be able to take off again with five people on board but he was forced to do as he was told. They took off again within seconds and flew north to the racecourse at Baldoyle.

The prisoners in the yard that day cheered and applauded the escapees as they rose into the sky. The warders, between thiry or forty in all, ran out of the main prison block once they realised what had happened. Some shouted for the main gate to be locked others just stood mesmerised by what was happening, totally powerless to prevent the escape. The helicopter touched down at Baldoyle where a car which had been taken in O'Connell Street earlier in the day, had been waiting to drive the men to safe houses. In later interviews it was revealed that some of the warders believed that the helicopter might have been the Minister for Defence arriving at the prison. This point was later taken up by the government's opposition in an emergency debate on security arising from the escape. "It is poetic justice," said Mr Lynch, the leader of the opposition, "that a helicopter is now at the heart of the Government's embarrassment and in the centre of their dilemma. Indeed it was hard to blame the prison officer who observed that he thought that the Minister for Defence was paying an informal visit to Mountjoy yesterday, because, of course, we all know that the Minister for Defence is wont to use helicopters, as somebody observed already, as other Ministers are wont to use State cars."

One prisoner who was closely involved in the planning and execution of the escape was Gerry O'Hare from Belfast. He takes up the story;

"That day dawned as any Hallowe'en day, or for that matter, any day at all. In the wing some fifty IRA prisoners were faced with their cold morning porridge. Things appeared normal and everybody went about their business in a relaxed mood. Keeping things relaxed was the name of the game. For just a handful of prisoners, myself included, knew that if things came off, there would be witches flying that night — three Provo witches.

"The idea of a helicopter escape had been aired before in other prisons and the Kesh but for reasons known only to those involved in their planning, they never came off. That September and October had been a bad time for the IRA. Several top members had been arrested by the Free State Government leading the then Taoiseach, Liam Cosgrave, to boast that his Government was having greater success than the British in crushing the movement. The decision to attempt the escape from Mountjoy was more than just logistical. It had a political input. Simply to make Cosgrave, his Fine Gael Party and the Labour Party with Conor Cruise O'Brien, eat their words.

"For several days before Hallowe'en we had been on a red alert, but something always seemed to delay the operation. Three prisoners had been chosen by the Army to escape, Seamus Twomey, J B O'Hagan and Kevin Mallon. Originally the number had been two escapees but that was changed to three by 'the outside escape committee', shortly before the event. Cosgrave had made much of their arrests so it seemed important to select high profile prisoners rather than others who were serving longer sentences. The choice had upset a few within the jail, but eventually they were consoled by the time-old principle that prisoners don't tell the Army outside how to run the campaign.

"Each of the handful of prisoners who were involved in the escape committee were told a few hours before the escape to select at least three other prisoners and take them into their confidence. Each small group had their instructions. Ours was to see that the three escapees succeeded in getting on board the helicopter and to thwart the efforts of the screws who would be trying to prevent it taking off again. Surprise was the key word.

"The usual afternoon entertainment was a football match. We had been told that during the game the helicopter would arrive. As we held the centre ground we could keep the screws on the outer boundary of the prison yard. Most of those playing were totally unaware of the drama that was to unfold. As the afternoon wore on (we were due to leave the yard at 4.15pm) the game also dragged on. A few of us kept encouraging those playing to keep it up. But, as things had to be seen to be normal, the game ended and the players dispersed back inside the wing. Those who had specific functions remained outside and a couple of us had to ask a few more to stay on in the yard. They were told simply, 'nudge nudge wink wink', that something was 'about to happen'.

"The escapees walked around the yard chatting normally, casting the odd glance in the air. Just as despondency was beginning to creep in we heard the unmistakable noise of the helicopter. It appeared low over the bottom of the yard and then moved away again. Our hearts sank, but in fact the pilot was aiming his approach and had to make a circular movement to line up his landing. Prison officers at first didn't think anything was amiss and everybody kept walking round the yard. Then and to this day I can't believe it — it was all over in one minute. The helicopter appeared over our heads and landed in the middle of the yard. The three escapees rushed forward — two entering from the right side and the third struggling to get in from the left.

"As this was happening the screws suddenly awoke to what was going on. The Volunteer in the front of the helicopter signalled to me to shut the back door as the third man couldn't turn to close the door himself. I rushed forward, slammed the door shut, and was nearly lifted upwards by the drag from the blades. There was dust swirling everywhere and as the helicopter slowly lifted upwards, it half turned and raced away over the low wall of the yard.

"All around me there was mayhem. Prison officers were grappling with prisoners, but most had been told to stay where they were and there would be no trouble. Most did. A few didn't. But it was too late. If I have one lasting memory of the escape it was the unfortunate screw who could be heard for minutes afterwards screaming, 'Close the f***ing gates. Close the f***ing gates', before the reality dawned on him that it would be no use as the escape was going up, not out."

The aftermath of this event was that all the political prisoners held in Mountjoy (except for Loyalists) were transferred to Portlaoise. Fearing a repetition at the Curragh the political prisoners there were also transferred to Portlaoise. The editor of *Der Spiegal* had an exclusive interview with Twomey shortly after his escape and claimed that people throughout Europe were calling the daring exploit 'the escape of the century.' Meanwhile the songwriters were busy composing the lyrics for yet another street ballad. 'The helicopter song' by the Wolfe Tones broke all

Dolphin Label sales records, while the popular Belfast-based group Wolfhound had thousands of their own record, 'the Provie Birdie' pressed and on the shelves within a week.

The Provie Birdie: McRobin

On the last day of October in the year of '73
In Mountjoy Jail three rebels were longing to be free,
When from the skies, surprise surprise
An iron bird did fall
And lifted up the Provies and took them over the wall

And its up and up and higher the helicopter flew
High over the Dublin Spires and over the Liffey too
The length and breadth of Ireland no finer sight did see
The day the Provie Birdie released the Mountjoy three

The following year Kenneth Littlejohn, inspired by the success of the republicans made his escape from Mountjoy Jail amid speculation that he was helped by other agencies. Kenneth Littlejohn had been a former paratrooper in the British Army and he went on to claim that both he and his brother Keith had been recruited as agents by MI6, a section of the British Secret Service. The Littlejohn brothers had been extradited from Britain to Ireland to stand trial for robbing the Allied Irish Bank in Grafton Street in October 1972. At the time they had got away with over £67,000. The robbery, they later claimed, was carried out in an attempt to discredit the IRA to try and force the Dublin Government to 'crack down more heavily on terrorist activity'. Both men received lengthy prison terms.

The argument as to whether or not they were agents and to what degree their espionage activities reached continues to be speculated upon to this day. What is known, is the fact that their extradition proceedings were held *in camera* for 'reasons of national security'. The two men ended up in Mountjoy but were kept in cells isolated from the other prisoners in the basement of the prison, for their own safety. At 7.30pm on 11 March 1974, both brothers managed to escape. They were seen scaling the walls by a warder who gave chase when they dropped into the street on the other side. Keith hurt his leg in the fall, and was recaptured after a fifty yard chase, but his brother Kenneth disappeared into the night.

Several days later Kenneth Littlejohn surfaced in Europe where he gave an interview with *Time Out* magazine giving details on how he escaped. Littlejohn revealed that he had made plans for his escape before he was extradited to Ireland to stand trial, knowing that he had no chance of getting off. He had concealed hacksaw blades in a tin of talcum powder which he brought with with him from jail in England.

While in the basement of Mountjoy he was allowed to practice yoga every day in a cell which he used specifically for that purpose. Littlejohn explained;

"I used to do yoga and I got everyone into the routine where for an hour or so every day I got the privacy to do my yoga. Because of the Irishman's respect for religion they regarded it as some sort of mythical religion, and of course, they would not intrude. In fact I was cutting the bars."

Littlejohn disclosed that he had gone on hunger strike to lose weight to enable him to squeeze through the window. The escape, he claimed, was almost foiled by a visit from his lawyer on the night they planned the breakout. The rope used was made out of blankets, which he had hidden in a punch bag to scale the outer wall. However, he dispensed with the rope and instead used some planks which builders had carelessly left lying at the bottom of the perimeter wall. They used these planks to get over the wall. He stood on Keith's shoulders to get up the wall and it was when he was on the top that he was spotted by a warder. Keith followed soon after him and they both made their way along the Royal Canal. As they got to the road, a car pulled up and a warder jumped out and tried to apprehend the two. Kenneth ran through a pub and after coming out the side door he boarded a bus. A sixth sense, he claimed, told him to get off and onto another one. His intuition was well founded because the first bus was stopped and searched. Littlejohn eventually hid under a boiler in a church. He was nearly caught by workmen the next day on several occasions. He then made his way to Howth Head where he lived in a bivouac for three days. He then made his way through Drogheda and continued on to Dundalk where he spent a couple of nights in "the best hotel in town."

He cut his hair to make himself look like an old man and took a train across the border to the port of Larne where he boarded the Stranraer ferry. It later emerged that a man from the British Embassy visited the Littlejohn brothers four days before their escape, but the British Government denied that they had any part in the escape, and that the visit was purely personal. The collusion theory raged for a long time afterwards, and demands for the resignation of the Minister for Justice and other top security officials came from the opposition. An internal inquiry found 'no collusion between staff and escapee'. Mountjoy has remained the scene of many incidents and disturbances since that time, but in the history of outstanding and memorable escapes, it has carved a niche for itself, as the jail from which the IRA escaped by helicopter — a scene which was almost re-enacted at Brixton several years later.

Belfast Jail and the prison yards from which many of the prisoners escaped.

8. Over the Wall.

Belfast Prison is situated on the City's Crumlin Road. Through time it has become known as Crumlin Road Jail or simply, 'the Crum'. It has featured prominently as a holding centre for Republican prisoners since its construction in 1845. It has been the home of thousands of young men from all over Ireland. During the Fenian Rising, William Harbinson died at the prison on 9 September 1867. The place was regarded as such an ornament of the town that it was featured prominently as a tourist attraction in the various guidebooks which were produced before the First World War. Directly facing the prison is the courthouse which has also been prominent in the penal history of the island. Both buildings are linked by an underground tunnel through which prisoners are manacled and brought for their court appearances.

Belfast prison was designed and built in the decade after the opening of Pentonville in London. Pentonville itself led in the furtherance of penal policy and administration, and at the time served as a model for more than fifty other prisons in Britain and Ireland. The basis of the architectural style of the prison was a semi-circular plan with wings, housing the cell blocks, radiating from a central control building. The idea behind such a plan was that a warder could see every wing and every landing and cell from one place, thereby reducing the manpower required to operate the prison.

The Victorian style of the building and the antique mode of administration was in use right up until its purpose was wound down in 1995. In the aftermath of the '1994 Ceasefire' 'the Crum's' use as a holding centre had been drastically reduced. From the first Fenians were interned there in the 1860s, right up until the 1990s, when the Diplock system of justice ensured that 'C' and 'A' Wings had a steady stream of 'long term' remand prisoners. It has been the scene of frequent controversy.

From the first Republican prisoners were housed there, 'the Crum' has been the scene of the government's continued attempts to treat political prisoners as common criminals. The failure of this policy led to different levels of negotiated regimes between the representatives of both the Republicans and the prison authorities down the years. It has only been since the early 1970s that the prison took on the appearance of a military installation, with reels of barbed wire, manned military observation posts and an aerial exclusion zone protected by military helicopters. The militarisation of 'the Crum' coincided with the development of the Territorial Army base which is situated behind it. This base began to house a regular British army battalion once the troops were shipped in to the North in 1969. It gradually developed into an important base in the British army's infrastructure in the North. The location of a military base adjoining the prison meant that the British military were always close at hand to subdue any disturbances which might occur at the jail. The militarisation of the prison coincided with the findings of numerous inquiries held in response to successful escapes all over the North. These inquiries advised more stringent control of political prisoners. The government could only go so far with their control policies realising that the only way they could ultimately control their prisoners would be to chain them to the floor. This had been tried against the Fenians, the most notable being O'Donovan Rossa, at Dartmoor prison, one hundred years previous. In the 1970's international media attention was focused on events in Northern Ireland. Images of war were flashed daily on television screens across the world. Groups such as Amnesty International, the Churches, the Irish Government and other interested bodies called for inquiries into the mistreatment of internees and prisoners. It was at this stage that the decision to build a special prison called HMP Maze Cellular was taken.

Most of the escapes from Crumlin Road prison are recalled in nationalist areas with great admiration and many have been remembered through ballads and songs. Nearly all of these escapes were effected by going over the wall, which proved to be the most effective way to get out of this grim Victorian building. Once the jail was heavily fortified, the Republican prisoners, not to be outdone, shot their way to freedom. The first escape of political prisoners from the jail did not happen, surprisingly, until 1927. After the general amnesty most political prisoners were released. There were several men who continued to be detained at Belfast Prison by the Northern Ireland government. Among them were, William Conlon from Gilford in County Down, Francis Boyle from Beragh in County Tyrone and Hugh Rogers from Sixmilecross, County Tyrone. All three had been charged with murder in 1920 and were eventually sentenced to life imprisonment, having been tried by a general court-martial at Victoria Barracks, Belfast on 20 April 1921. Realising that the government were intent on holding them hostage until they served their full sentences, the three decided to escape. With the help of another prisoner named Edward Thornton, they arranged to go over the wall on the night of 9 May 1921. The prisoners managed to jam the bolt on their cell door, then, after lock-up that night, they carefully opened the door and thereby gained access to the landing. Here they overpowered the night guard and after tying him up and relieving him of his revolver and keys they let themselves out into the exercise yard. The rest of the escape was then quite easy to accomplish. The prisoners threw a makeshift rope ladder up over the wall and climbed to freedom. A car had been arranged to wait on the road to pick them up, and with all four passengers safely inside the car sped down the Crumlin Road. An RUC man was on point duty that night in Donegall Street. He told an enquiry, which was held after the escape, that he heard the sound of a speeding car getting louder and louder. When it came into view he noticed that its headlights were out. He claimed that it drove straight for him and he just managed to jump out of its path as it sped past. The only description he had of the car was that it was red. With this tiny bit of information the police began their investigations and the search was on to try and recapture the escapees. Homes and businesses were raided on the Falls Road, where the police believed they had gone to ground and a £500 reward was offered to entice potential informers, but the escapers like many before them and many afterwards got away.

The 1930's were traumatic times for Belfast, as the loyalist pogroms continued where they had left off in the early 1920's. No sooner had the killings subsided than the Second World War started. Those unfortunate enough to be targeted as suspected subversives, were rounded up and interned in Crumlin Road. The 1927 escape was still fresh in many peoples' memories and before long a similar escape plan was put together again. Stories reached the prisoners of the fate of their counterparts in the South 'while trying to escape'. John Kavanagh was shot dead at a tunnel at Cork Jail in August 1940, while Barney Casey was shot dead at the Curragh that December. Added to that were the deaths of Republican hunger strikers Tony D'Arcy and Seán MacNeela at Mountjoy in the same year and the executions of other republican leaders. On the morning of 5 June 1941 five internees, four from Belfast and one from Derry, escaped. They had been interned without trial in the Belfast Prison, the authorities believing that their presence on the streets in the North would be too great a security risk during the war. The prison housed many of the government's suspects and it is reported that the atmosphere was tense and claustrophobic as German bombers blitzed the entire city, killing over one thousand people in one night and destroying many of the buildings in and around the prison. It was said that the blitz was one of the main incidents to prompt the escape but it was obvious that the escape had been planned in advance. A rope and grappling hook having previously been made by the prisoners, it was decided to go over the wall during the exercise period. As the men forced open a gap in the corrugated iron hoarding the view of the warders was blocked by the other internees. Over one hundred prisoners were reported to have aided the escape even though only five actually got away. More might have reached the outside but for the swift action of the prison guards who realised that an escape was taking place almost as soon as the hook hit the top of the wall. The plan was to slip through the hole in the railings before climbing the twenty foot perimeter wall at the back of the jail. However, hopes that many more would be getting out were suddenly dashed when the alarm was sounded. Only five went over the top. One man was hauled from the rope by warders and two others were caught as they wriggled their way under the fence.

The five men who escaped were, Phil Taggart, Liam Burke, Paddy Watson, Eddie Keenan and Gerry Doherty. It was reported that when the warders eventually realised who had escaped and went to their cells, Gerry Doherty, from Derry's Brandywell, had written on the wall "The Bird has flown." Doherty was nicknamed 'The Bird' and the authorities were reported to have gone into a rage.

Meanwhile, Dr John Harrington, who was one of the few people in Belfast to have a car was just turning in to the Mater Hospital when the five men came rushing down the driveway between the hospital and the jail. Harrington, in an interview many years later recalled the scene. He said he knew immediately that something was wrong and recalled, "On the braces of one was a Sacred Heart badge as large as an onion." Harrington opened the car door and said, "get in." All five were brought to a safe house in Belfast, where they were to lie low for a week or so, before they were moved to the border on the occasion of a major Gaelic football match in Armagh.

Following the escape of the internees morale was high at the jail. That sense of joy was soon to be dampened when, in 1942 six young Belfast men were eventually sentenced to death for shooting dead Patrick Murphy, a member of the RUC, who chased after them into a house in Cawnpore Street. One of the six, Thomas Joseph Williams, was hanged at the jail on 2 September 1942. Four months later events at the prison were making headlines yet again.

On 15 January 1943, another escape was made from the prison. Of the four who got away one was the IRA's Chief of Staff, Hugh McAteer. All four men were serving long sentences at the time. The news made for sensational reading in the following day's papers. At the time there were three hundred internees and up to three hundred remand and sentenced prisoners being held at the jail. At 8.30am, while the rest of the prisoners were preparing to have their breakfast, the four escapees were scaling the back wall. The men went to the third floor toilets at the end of the landing at 'A' Wing where they had arranged to assemble once the warders' attention had been distracted. While there they hauled themselves up through a trap door in the ceiling. From the roofspace they were able to break a hole in the roof and gain access to the perimeter wall which they quickly scaled using a rope ladder made from sheets taken from their cells. A car which had been waiting outside drove them off to freedom. The identities of the four were soon wired to all the police stations around the North and a security cordon was erected around the City to try and capture their 'most wanted men.'

The four were Hugh McAteer, a book-keeper from Derry, who was serving fifteen years for treason; Jimmy Steele, a Belfastman, who was serving ten years for possession of a revolver and documents; Patrick Donnelly, a Portadown man, who was serving twelve years; and Ned Maguire, another Belfastman, who was serving six years. A substantial reward of £3,000 was offered for the recapture of any or all of the men. Ned Maguire and Patrick Donnelly remained free until the end of the war.

The prison had been relatively quiet for the period after the war. Internees were gradually released but with the commencement of the 'Border Campaign' in the mid Fifties a new wave of internees once again ended up behind the bars at 'the Crum'. Before long the courts began to sentence various people with charges relating to this campaign and they too ended up in the jail at Belfast. Security measures were tightened at the prison. One of the measures which was implemented was the construction of watch towers in the corners of the jail. On 6 June, 1957, three 'non-political' prisoners escaped from the complex whilst carrying out these new fortifications. Subsequently security was tightened and then in May the following year a statement was issued by the Government Press Office.

> *An attempted escape on the part of the internees in Belfast Prison was foiled by the vigilance of the prison staff.*
> *The behaviour of certain internees had for some time aroused the suspicion of the officers in charge of the internees, and a special watch was kept on their movements.*
> *As a consequence of this watch the officers discovered that a tunnel was in the course of construction through which, no doubt, in due course the internees hoped to make their escape from the prison.*

As a result of the discovery, the internees lost privileges and visits were cancelled as security at the prison was tightened even further. The discovery of the tunnel led to the favoured method of escape — scaling the prison wall. This, however, is not how the first escape from the jail was accomplished. In 1901 a burglar escaped from the stone yard at the back of the prison by running out through a gate as a delivery cart entered.

The next attempt to break out was in 1960. On that occasion two men, Sean Kelly and Daniel Donnelly, made their jump for freedom. In the time honoured fashion of going over the wall the two planned to escape on Boxing Day. Only one succeeded however. Donnelly got over first and as Kelly was following close behind the rope snapped. He fell back into the yard, injuring his foot. He was charged with attempted escape and lost whatever privileges he was due and did not get released until 1963. The last internee left 'the Crum' on 25 April 1961. Those who were sentenced remained in prison until they had served the term of their sentence.

With the escalation of the conflict in August 1969 another batch of prisoners filled 'the Crum'. Very quickly the prison system was overwhelmed. Internment camps were opened at Long Kesh and Magilligan and as British Troops were drafted in from other British military bases across Europe, the scenes of war and the associated hostilities flashed up on newscreens all over the world. Belfast resembled the battle scenes of Europe in the Second World War. Before long the tunnellers and planners were down to work. Escape committees were formed. In the confusion and disorder of this latest wave of civil strife, it was still relatively easy to escape from the jail and in the well-honoured tradition the men simply procured a rope, organised transport, scaled the walls and got away.

In June 1971 James McCann loosened the bars of his cell in 'C' Wing and lowered himself on to a rope made of sheets into the yard. Known as 'the Fox', he evaded capture until he was arrested in Kildare several years later. Internment was introduced in August of that year and the prison population grew overnight. In the first week of internment one hundred and twenty four men were locked up in 'C' Wing of the jail.

Three months later nine men carved a name for themselves in the history books as 'The Crumlin Kangaroos' when they scaled the wall during a football match The audacity of the escapees was celebrated in a ballad which was being sung around the North even before the escapees themselves had found a safe billet in which to go to ground.

The subsequent clampdown by the warders was defied by the cool and unnerved escape two weeks later of three others, Martin Meehan, Dutch Doherty and Hugh McCann. The authorities were reeling with embarrassment as internal inquiries were set up to find out what went wrong and how to prevent the same thing happening in the future. The Compton Report which had been set up to allay public fears over allegations of mistreatment at the time, had yet another embarrassing report to cover as many of those who escaped later made statements to the press about their ill-treatment at the hands of the British Army. One of those who went on record about his ill-treatment and his subsequent successful escape was Ardoyne Republican, Martin Meehan. He takes up the story;

"I was arrested on the 9 November, 1971. I got a severe beating by the British Army and received forty-seven stitches to the back of my head. To save me from further brutality I pretended I was unconscious and I ended up in the hospital. I was in a bad way but I was still conscious of what was going on around me. Anyway after getting the stitches I was taken to Holywood Barracks on a stretcher. Holywood was a notorious torture centre at the time. Most people were brought out of Holywood Barracks on stretchers but with me it was the other way around. While there I was put through a very degrading and brutal interrogation after which they brought me down to Crumlin Road Jail where I was detained.

"I was there a week when 'the Crumlin Kangaroos' escaped during a football match. The first thing everyone said after that was, 'Well that's it, no one is ever going to get out of here again'. The screws closed everything down for two weeks while army engineers moved in to make the prison more secure. At that time the remand prisoners were in 'B' Wing while the detainees were held in 'C' Wing. Eventually they let us out to play a Gaelic match and they let three spectators out with us. I was on a walking stick at the time. I was supposed to be one of the linesmen. I remember that me and a fella called Micky Maguire were walking around the side of the pitch. Micky's father, Ned Maguire, escaped in the 1940's. We passed over this manhole cover and we heard it rattle. On further examination we realised that it went down to a depth of about six feet and had a pool of water in the bottom. We were not sure how deep the water was but we soon hatched an escape plan. There were screws surrounding the pitch with walkie talkies and there were armed soldiers in the pill boxes. There were now barbed wire fences and corrugated iron fences all the way round the pitch so that you couldn't get anywhere near the perimeter wall. We began to talk about it and throw some ideas about. We eventually came to the conclusion that if we could get into the manhole at half time and stay there until nightfall then maybe we would have a chance of reaching the perimeter wall and getting over it like the lads had done the previous fortnight. It was a chance in a million. When we put it to the OC he had grave reservations about the plot but after a lot of coaxing he eventually conceded and so the plan swung into motion.

"We made a rope out of sheets. We then made a three pronged hook out of the legs of a chair and bandaged it with sheets to muffle the sound as it hit the wall. Then somebody came up with the suggestion that we should cover ourselves from head to toe with a pound of butter so as to protect us from the cold and damp. We overlooked the problems this would cause whenever we tried to climb the rope. We kept sliding back down again because our hands were that slippery. At half time during a gaelic match on 2 December, we acted on our plan. The lads formed a half circle while some of the other lads distracted the screws. We opened the lid and me and Dutch Doherty dropped in. We had ropes around our waists just in case the water in the hole was too deep. There was only enough room for the two of us and we were up to our necks in ice cold water. Then another lad called Hugh McCann climbed in on top of us. He was not supposed to go on the escape but he got into the manhole and the lid was placed back over us. It was a tight squeeze. McCann was resting on our shoulders and it was very uncomfortable. Meanwhile up above, the lads continued with the match. Some of the lads feigned injury and took their places on the sidelines to cover for us. The screws fell for it, as not only were they anxious to get away for their dinner but it was pay day into the bargain and they were more interested in looking at their pay cheques than watching us playing football. We had to stay for six hours down the manhole. While down there we heard the lads go off and shortly afterwards we heard another batch of prisoners, this time YPs (Young Prisoners) playing a football match.

"Back at the wing the lads had confused the screw doing the count by messing about, pushing and shoving while going back into the wing. This ploy was continued at tea time with the effect that the screws did not even notice that we were missing. We also had it arranged that we wouldn't have any visits from our wives or our solicitors. Then at around 6.00pm we opened the lid. To our surprise, and to our advantage, a fog had dropped and it was so thick that you could barely see six to seven yards in front of you. It suited us because it meant that the pill boxes were rendered out of order. You can imagine the state of us having been submerged in the water for that length of time in December. It was bitterly cold and we tried to bring some life back into our bodies before crawling around the side of the pitch. We crawled beneath the barbed wire fence and made our way to the wall at the side of Girdwood Barracks. We were cut to pieces. As we were moving along I said to the two lads, 'Hold it hold it, I think we're caught.' There in front was a soldier pointing his rifle directly at us. We crouched down and I said I was making a run for it. As I got closer to the soldier I found out that it was a cement mixer with the handle still sticking out of it. Well, we had a good chuckle at that. We were lucky that we made our run between dog patrols. When we got to the wall we threw the rope up several times before it eventually caught. I went up first followed by Hugh McCann. When we were on top of the wall I slid over to one side and Hugh McCann slid over to the other side to make way for Dutch. The place we chose dropped into an alleyway between Cliftonpark Avenue and the jail. Anyhow we let ourselves down the other side in the same order. I remember shouting up to Dutch, 'Come on, hurry up' and when I looked round he was standing beside me. He had jumped off the wall because a searchlight was coming round. It was a thirty foot drop but luckily he didn't hurt himself.

"We had arranged for a green Avenger to be parked in Cliftonpark Avenue with the keys in the ignition and there it was. The car eventually started as the engine had been cold and we drove down towards Agnes Street and across to the Falls and down into McDonnell Street to my mother-in-law's house. We were black from head to toe. Once here, we were swiftly taken to safe houses. I got over the border that Sunday. I was driving a car with a young woman and a child as passengers. The UDR stopped me and I remember saying 'What's the problem?' and he said 'Ach its them three bastards escaped the other night. I'm standing out here. It's a waste of time.' I replied 'Sure you never know your luck!"

Nine months later Martin Meehan was captured in Jamaica Street and was charged with escaping from lawful custody while on remand. Meehan conducted his own defence and argued that under the Special Powers Act a British soldier had no power of arrest. This line of defence concluded that all the detainees who were arrested by the British Army were being held illegally and as such he had the lawful right to escape. Lord Justice McGonigle agreed with this argument and awarded Meehan £800 for being held illegally for twenty-three days prior to escaping. In true British fashion the Parliament passed a law overnight to legalise the detention of all the other detainees from the moment of their arrest.

Over the wall, over the wall
Who would believe they jumped over the wall
Over the wall, over the wall
Its hard to believe they went over the wall

Now the warders looked on with the greatest surprise
And the sight that they saw brought tears to their eyes
For one of the teams was not there at all
They all got transferred and went over the wall.

Now the governor came down with his face in a twist
Said, "Line up these lads while I check me list"
But nine of the lads didn't answer the call
And the warder said, "Please, sir, they're over the wall."

The security forces were shook to the core
So they barred every window and bolted each door
But all their precautions were no use at all
For another three prisoners went over the wall

On 13 January 1973, Daniel Keenan fooled the warders by escaping disguised as another prisoner who was due for release. Then on 22 February 1973, a man named Jim Bryson made his own daring escape. Bryson had been a well-known Republican activist from the Ballymurphy area of Belfast. He had been detained on the *Maidstone* in 1971 when he swam ashore with six others several weeks after being arrested. He was arrested again in September 1972 for possession of a revolver and was put on remand and held in Long Kesh. It was when he was transferred to Crumlin Road for court hearings that he planned his escape with dexterity and boldness. The Courthouse where the prisoners had to appear was directly facing the jail and prisoners were escorted to the building via an underground tunnel. On that particular day Bryson was led along the tunnel along with three other s. While in the cells below the court Bryson pulled a gun on the warder, tied him up and after donning his uniform Bryson and another prisoner, Malachy McCarry made off through the courthouse. McCarry was recaptured but Bryson succeeded in getting away.

Bryson's story does not end there because it is said that once outside he headed towards the Shankill Road where he flagged down a car, telling the occupants that his wife had just been rushed to the Royal Victoria Hospital. It later turned out that the men in the car were off-duty UDR soldiers.

The gun which Bryson used had been brought in months earlier with a view to helping four men make their getaway dressed as prison tradesmen. The plan was to approach one of the pill boxes at the back of the prison while dressed in overalls and pretending that they had been sent to fix one of the searchlights, gain access to the pill box, and overpower the sentry. Things went wrong however and the plans had to be abandoned. The gun was hidden quite safely in a dump within the jail. When Jim Bryson saw the opportunity of escaping from the Courthouse he retrieved the weapon and used it to effect his own escape. His freedom did not last long and he was shot dead by the British Army on 31 August that same year.

Another escape attempt which had to be abandoned in 1973 involved a tunnel from Landscape Terrace, a street beside the jail. The IRA had a four man team digging a tunnel from the kitchen of a house in the street towards the canteen in 'A' Wing. Plans had to be abandoned whenever the British Army arrived at the front door following a tip off and discovered the tunnel. The men in 'A' Wing were making their preparations to go as the tunnel had been in under the jail when it was discovered. Security at the jail was tightened even further when a woman visitor was arrested after she had allegedly left a clothes parcel in to the jail in October 1973. The soles of a pair of platform shoes had been hollowed out. A gun along with ammunition was concealed in one , while the other was weighted to give an equal balance. The parcel never got past the search area. Many other plans either had to be abandoned or were deemed much too dangerous to proceed with by the IRA staff in the jail. Nevertheless the watching and scheming continued.

The next successful escape from the prison was carried out by a group of men dubbed 'The M60 Team.' The M60 was the latest edition to the Belfast Brigade's arsenal in the late 1970's. It had been designed for use by the US Army and because of its rapid fire mechanism, British security forces did their utmost to capture the guns from the IRA. By the Spring of 1981 several men were before the Belfast Diplock Courts on charges arising from the alleged use of these heavy machine guns. The day before they were to be sentenced they broke out of the prison and yet another carefully planned escape was crowned with success.

1981 is probably best remembered for the tragic H-Block hunger strike. By June of that year four men had already died, Bobby Sands, Francis Hughes, Patsy O'Hara and Ray McCreesh. The hunger strike was still continuing although at that stage none of the other hunger strikers were at a critical stage. Outside feelings were tense. The Twenty Six County elections were due on 11 June and several of the hunger strikers had been put forward as candidates. On the day before the election the regime inside Crumlin Road Jail began like every other day. The prison had been the scene of several protests regarding strip-searching shortly beforehand, but the rules were eventually relaxed. On 'A' and 'C' Wings the remand prisoners were outside in the yard for exercise. Several men from each wing, as was a usual occurrence, were called for visits. Some of these visits were from solicitors and an area of the prison was set aside to allow legal teams and the accused to discuss their business in private. Having successfully managed to be on a legal visit at the same time eight men quickly overpowered the warders in that section of the jail. For around thirty minutes eight Republican prisoners took full control of the visiting area using a selection of small arms. After locking the warders in holding cells and ensuring the safety of several civilians caught up in the drama they left the prison buildings dressed as solicitors and warders. Once outside however the alarm was set off and the British Army opened fire on the prisoners from a watchtower before they could reach the front gate. Undeterred the prisoners continued with their plan. Outside the prison, cars had previously been parked in the car park of the health clinic beside the courthouse, their ignition keys hidden under the floor mats. The prisoners ran across the road towards the health centre at the same time dodging bullets as they went. Taking the same route as Bryson had done almost ten years earlier the escapees headed towards the Loyalist Shankill area where they hijacked cars to help their getaway. All eight men reached safe houses within the hour and after a lying low for a short while they were spirited over the border to begin new lives 'on the run.' The eight men were Anthony Sloan and his brother Gerry, Angelo Fusco, Michael McKee, Robert Campbell, Paul Magee, Pete Ryan and Joe Doherty.

One of the many remand prisoners interviewed about the incident recalls the excitement that ensued as he was caught up in the M60 escape.

"I was in 'the Crum' on remand during the 1981 hunger strikes. The jail was the scene of many protests. The men had all been psyching themselves up for going on the blanket once they were sentenced but at the back of everyone's mind was the hope that a solution would be found before long. Once the first hunger strike was called off only to be followed by a second one we had a gut feeling that there would be deaths. A form of segregation had already been agreed upon by the time I was sent to the Crum. 'A' and 'C' Wings housed the remand prisoners while 'B' Wing housed short-term and 'D' Wing long-term sentenced prisoners. Most of these were in for ordinary crimes of a non political nature. As the hunger strikers began to die morale was very low. After Raymond McCreesh died I remember being brought down for a legal visit. About ten of us were brought down together that Wednesday to the visiting rooms where we were to meet our solicitors in private rooms. We were placed in large cells together before being brought to the consultation rooms. Others were already there from 'A' Wing. Once they were let out to see the solicitor the lads took over the place.

"I realised what was happening when Pete Ryan appeared at the consultation room door dressed in a screw's uniform. He said "Well what do you think?" He definitely looked the part. Pete was the only man who was not up on a charge with the M60 team. He was eventually to die in a hail of bullets at Coagh on 3 June 1991. We were brought back round and, apologising for having to lock us in, we were placed back in the holding cells which by this stage was full of screws, some in a state of partial undress, solicitors and other prisoners. Everyone did as instructed. Part of the take-over involved securing the 'B' Wing visiting area and visitors and prisoners were brought to the holding cells. Just when they had everyone in the cells there was near disaster. A screw came down the steps from the prison proper to the gate where the legal visits were held. He had a prisoner in front of him from our wing, the OC of the INLA. "Legals, One on." he shouted through the grille. Little did he know that not three yards in front of him stood about ten screws, all of whom had been taken hostage. One of the lads who had been dressed in a screw's uniform opened the gate and the screw, not recognising the prisoner in uniform, came on in. Once the gate closed behind him a gun was put to his head and he was also taken hostage and along with his prisoner he was put into the holding cell. The screw at the top of the steps was none the wiser and didn't realise what was happening out at the legals.

"Then just as they were about to make a break for it a woman took ill. One of the lads sent for a glass of water and even got her a cigarette. The woman was unimpressed with this chivalrous behaviour and said to him, "Look son never mind me, just hurry up and do what you have to do." Time was running out and before long the eight men made their getaway. I heard the shooting just after they left and immediately thought things had gone wrong. There was a period of silence and then after about five or ten minutes we could hear dogs barking and doors slamming. The screws and police were back in control of the building again. They began counting the prisoners and I could hear them telling one another that the rest had got away. The screws and other hostages were released and we discussed between ourselves what might happen to us. We couldn't believe it when we were escorted to our cells without first receiving a beating. I even had time to go tell the OC that all the lads had got safely away. It must have been an instruction they had because of the hunger strike. We were all locked in our cells for two days and visits were cancelled while a search of the jail was carried out. Everyone was up at the windows discussing what had happened.

"A couple of days later there was this fella brought in from up the country for 'keeping gear'. He had only been charged and was out on his first visit. After about an hour or so he came back to the wing and was let out to the yard to join the rest of us. He brought back startling news. At the end of his visit it appeared that he was escorted back through the visiting area with his visitors. The final gate was opened to him and when he saw a bus on the Crumlin Road. He told the screw that he must've went the wrong way and was escorted back to the wing. So much for all the security restrictions. By the time the story had went round everyone was watching for chances to get out."

There were many more attempts to break free from the walls of Crumlin Road before it finally closed its doors in April 1995 having served its purpose as a detention centre for one hundred and fifty-one years.

Derry Jail, Bishop Street. *(Courtesy of National Museum, Kildare Street)*

9. Derry's Walls.

Derry Jail was ripped down in 1971 after serving as a holding centre for prisoners from that county since 1824. The jail officially closed in March 1953. It stood in the City's Bishop Street and there had never been a recorded escape from that institution until Frank Carty arrived there in 1920. He was one of the most successful jail breakers in Ireland and was the Brigadier of Sligo's No.4 Brigade. Born in 1897, he joined the Irish Volunteers in 1914 and first escaped in June 1920 from Sligo Jail. Six feet tall and of athletic build he commanded an air of authority and his subsequent promotion to Brigadier was well founded. After his rescue from the jail in Sligo he took command of a flying column but his leadership was short-lived for, after only five months he was captured along with two others, at Moylough in Tobercurry by the Black and Tans. Shot in the wrist, he was taken and incarcerated in Derry Jail which at the time had housed many other IRA prisoners under the strictest security. This security however had been compromised and through the cooperation of several warders a regular line of communication was opened between Republican hostages and the IRA on the outside.

After the winter, Derry's Charlie McGuinness soon made contact with Frank Carty and before long an escape plan swung into operation. This plan was not sanctioned by the IRA and was the single-handed plan of McGuinness himself, a close compatriot of Carty's and a native of Derry's Pennyburn area. Carty was instructed to get himself transferred to the hospital wing of the jail. While there he would cut a hole in the bars with the use of a smuggled hacksaw. By this method he would then be able to drop down into the yard into which a rope ladder would be thrown so he could scale the wall. The jail wall abutted on to the back-yards of the houses in Harding Street.

Carty succeeded in the first part of the plan and was soon in a cell in the hospital wing sawing away through the bars. No easy task by any means, but perseverance and the desire for freedom spurred him on. He filled the gaps in the bars with a mixture of soap and dust and then calmly waited for the morning of Saturday 12 February to approach, the date of the planned escape.

At 4.00am McGuinness was standing alone in the backyard of a house in Harding Street. Taking several attempts to secure the grappling hook onto the top of the wall he finally succeeded in making it catch. Tugging on the rope to make sure it was firm he scrambled up. Half-way up disaster struck. The coping of the old jail gave way and McGuinness, the rope ladder and finally the coping came crashing down with a tremendous thud which echoed through the winter air. McGuinness thought it best to gave up for the time being anyway. Carty waited patiently at his cell window. Not receiving the signal he retired to his bunk dejected.

The next day however Carty's spirits were raised again when a warder approached him and slipped him a ball of twine and a note explaining that the escape was postponed until 15 February at 4.30am. Carty this time was to throw the ball of twine over the perimeter wall from his cell window, keeping hold of the loose end. The morning of the escape soon arrived and once again McGuinness took his position in the backyard of a house in Harding Street while Carty managed to accurately throw the ball of twine down to him. A tug on the twine gave the signal that the rope had been securely tied to the end and Carty reeled the rope up through the bars of his cell. He secured the rope to a solid window bar and after pushing the sawn bars to the side he squeezed his hefty form out of the window and shimmied down the rope into the backyard of Moore's house. Out through the front door they immediately headed for Abercorn Place and on to the relative safety of the Strand.

The escape was not discovered until 7.00am. The RIC and Military were furious at the successful escape of Carty and they immediately swamped Derry in a search operation. The police were still raiding homes in their vain search when Carty was disembarking from the collier *Carricklee* at Glasgow.

He was not long in Glasgow when he was captured again. This time the IRA planned to rescue him. A meeting was held and it was agreed that they would attack the Black Maria which would return Carty to the Glasgow Jail after his court appearance. The IRA took up their positions and, at a given signal, attacked the van as it slowed to enter the prison. A Police Inspector named Johnston who was guarding the prisoner fell dead, shot through the heart as he drew his pistol to open fire. A gunbattle ensued as the prison van raced out of the street. The rescue attempt had failed and Carty was returned to jail where he was sentenced to ten years' penal servitude. He was transferred to Mountjoy jail in Dublin where he remained until after the Treaty was signed.

On 2 December 1921 an escape attempt which went drastically wrong ended with the death of two police constables named William Lyttle and James Gorman. As a result three men were sentenced to death.

Derry Jail remained in the news and, as the twenties unfolded a new Treaty was signed and a separate government was established on the island of Ireland. Several days before the Treaty was signed, another daring escape was nearly accomplished at Derry. The men involved in that attempt were tried at the Spring Assizes in March 1922 and received sentences of six months each. On 31 August 1922 another attempt at escape was foiled, this time a tunnel was discovered.

In 1923, a hunger strike for the unconditional release of all internees on the prison ship Argenta, led to the prisoners on that ship being transferred to the Derry prison. Internment was eventually phased out in 1924. As the twenties eased into the thirties the Wall Street Crash had repercussions throughout the world. After the Hunger riots in the North came the Second World War. The government undertook a mass swoop against Republicans all over the North on 22 December 1938, three days before Christmas. Throughout 1939 several other swoops were made and the internees were dispersed in prisons throughout the North. The Free State Government also introduced internment.

In October 1939 the protests against internment without trial took a dramatic upsurge with a mutiny in Derry Jail. Forty-five prisoners overpowered warders in the exercise yard and barricaded themselves in a corridor for several hours. The 'B' Specials were immediately summoned to the scene and with the help of the Fire Brigade suppressed the disturbance.

Following the mutiny, a prison ship project which had been previously adopted by the Northern Ireland Government in 1922, was revived. This time a four thousand ton steamer named *Al Rawdah* was chartered from the Ministry of Shipping and was fitted with three hundred cells and accommodation for warders and a Governor. Two thousand internees were transferred amid a rigid security operation. To prevent anybody escaping from this hulk some extraordinary precautions were taken. Armoured cars escorted the buses to the coast while troops guarded the streets around the prison by erecting barbed wire entanglements. A fleet of small craft conveyed the men from the dock out to the ship. Because of mounting pressure on the government about deteriorating conditions on this prison hulk the authorities decided to close the jail.

Liam Burke was a Belfastman who had previously escaped from the Crumlin Road

Prison in 1941. Having been 'on the run' he made a tragic mistake by returning to his hometown of Belfast in 1942. He was captured again and was imprisoned for a short time on the *Al Rawadah*. Burke was recorded as the prime mover in Derry Jail's most notable breakout on 20 March 1943. On this occasion, along with twenty other internees he escaped in a furniture van in a scene which was to be repeated years later at the Maze Prison in 1983.

In the spring of 1943 the Allied Advance against Nazi Germany was headline news as people read of the far off battles of Rommel and General Eisenhower. Back home, however, another battle of wits was being acted out at the Derry and Donegal border. Saint Patrick's Day was a Wednesday that year and Derry Gaol's internees had muted celebrations. The following day the number of internees at the jail was supplemented by the arrival of more men from Belfast. This brought the prison's population up to two hundred and fifty and more staff were drafted in to guard the extra prisoners. That number was soon to change in what turned out to be the biggest ever escape from a Northern Ireland Prison at that time. The prisoners had been planning an escape for months and before long the day of the escape, Saturday 20 March, arrived. The plot had been carefully coordinated with the IRA on the outside. Jimmy Steele, who had escaped from Belfast Prison in January, 1943, hired a furniture van and driver in Belfast. Once they arrived in Derry City the driver was overpowered and kidnapped.

Inside the prison the internees who had been tunnelling for some time had reached the rear of a house in Harding Street and ended in a coal shed in the yard. The tunnel was about forty yards long and was started in a cell on the ground floor of the prison. The cell had a wooden floor and it was quite a simple operation to replace the floor boards to hide the tunnel's entrance. The shaft was sunk to a depth of twelve feet before the burrowing started in earnest. The prisoners had to shift around five tons of clay and they took full advantage of the fact that, not only was the sewer system of the jail very deep but in fact it also had a very efficient flushing system. On entering the coal shed a total of twenty-one men, dashed through the house and onto the street within three or four minutes,.

The furniture van, which had been driven from Belfast, was waiting at the corner of Abercorn Place and it was in this van that the men were spirited away. Several machine guns were left in the van to help the men secure a safe passage out of Derry. A young girl, named Logue, through whose house the escapees ran, was interviewed the following day by a local newspaper. She stated,

> *I was preparing breakfast in the scullery when the door suddenly opened and a number of young men, their clothes bespattered with clay, dashed in. For a moment I was speechless. Then I ordered*

*them out and the intruders, without making any comment ran into
the hall.*

The furniture van sped out of Derry and headed for the Donegal border. At the border the van stopped and seven men got out. Meanwhile back in Derry, a young girl, who had been passing in the street noticed the men scrambling into the back of the van. She rushed up and alerted the guards on the front gate of the prison. Once the alarm was raised the RUC put roadblocks up on all roads leading out of the City. On the other side of the border a cordon had not yet been set up to capture the internees. The Customs officers at Carrigans notified the Gardaí that the furniture van had passed that way and a number of Gardaí tried unsuccessfully to stop it as it passed through the village. They initially believed that the van was part of a smuggling operation. When the news of the escape had been wired to them they soon realised what was really happening and it was quite easy to follow the prisoners in the direction in which they travelled. All twenty men were in the van at this stage and when the van stopped on a second-class road two or three hundred yards from Kinnacally Mountain everyone got out. The passengers lost little time in making themselves scarce and the vehicle made its way back in the St Johnston direction. When the internees alighted they quickly made their way to the mountains. Some two hours later, army trucks with fully equipped military personnel and accompanied by Gardaí officers, arrived at the scene. They spread out fanwise to commence the three hundred feet ascent of the mountain. With the combined forces of police and military they worked wearily inwards until at the end of five hours twelve internees were taken in to custody. All twelve were unarmed and upon rearrest they were transferred to the Curragh internment camp where they remained until the end of the war.

A Home Office inquiry, conducted by Sir Charles Wickham, Inspector General of the RUC, was immediately opened at the jail. The jailbreak was the biggest ever known in the Six Counties. Nine men were still unaccounted for. One of the internees, a Belfast man, did not make it in time and was left in the street. He was recaptured on the Letterkenny Road half a mile from the city thirty-six hours later. It was believed that up to eighty men had planned to go out on the escape but that only the first batch of men made it due to the young girl raising the alarm.

Some of those who escaped were Brendan O'Boyle (who later died in a premature explosion outside Stormont on 2 July 1955); Seamus Burns (who was shot dead in Belfast on 12 February 1944); Liam Graham; Eddie Steel; John McGreevy; and James O'Hagan.

Magilligan Camp first hit the headlines when it became a centre for interrogation by the British Army and RUC Special Branch. Situated at a picturesque beauty spot twenty-five miles North-West of Derry at Castlerock, it was finally used as an internment camp in January 1972. The camp had only opened when the government stepped up their actions against Civil Rights activists. Derry was singled out for special treatment. On 22 January 1972, an anti-internment march was attacked by Paratroopers as the protesters approached the camp along the beach. Shortly afterwards the world's press descended on the North. On 30 January, that same year, another anti-internment march took place on what was later to be known as 'Bloody Sunday.' On this occasion up to thirty unarmed civilians were shot as they fled from a carefully orchestrated attack by the Paratroopers. Fourteen men were fatally injured. Magilligan gradually developed with the prisoners *in situ* and soon resembled the internment camp at Long Kesh.

The location of the camp at Magilligan meant that tunnelling was virtually impossible due to the high water level. Be that as it may, the moles were soon down at work. At one stage a seventy foot tunnel was discovered. Indeed, it took a certain type of psyche to engage in such a daunting task, as the danger of being buried alive was a constant reality. Like those who engaged in tunnelling at the Curragh and Long Kesh, the tunnells burrowed out of the camp through seams of sand. Not one of the tunnels at Magilligan camp were successful but several people still did escape. In 1975 Daniel Keenan managed to escape. Two months later on 7 May 1975, Peadar O'Hagan and Paddy McCann got away and the following year Martin Monaghan escaped disguised as a teacher to be followed in 1977 by Denis McFeely and Paul Butler also managed to break out. During one of the many raids at the camp on 16 May 1975 the British Army discovered two separate tunnels. One which was fifty-seven feet long led from the Republican cages, while the other, which was thirty-five feet long, led from the Loyalist cages. Both parties were digging towards the perimeter.

In 1980 three H-Blocks were built at Magilligan and the jail was used in a Government policy to isolate Republican prisoners, and therefore undermine their staff structures, which had been organised throughout the H-Blocks after the hunger strikes. Magilligan housed short term prisoners and the security regime within the Camp was similar to that implemented at Long Kesh. Following a series of explosive and ammunition finds coupled with sustained protests, all Republican prisoners were eventually housed at Maze Cellular.

10. Great Sporting Moments.

The Irish love of sport is renowned throughout the world. Many of the world's greatest athletes have come from Ireland and some of the best known football players have also done their country proud. This love of sport is reflected in some of the most memorable escapes to have taken place throughout Ireland's history.

It is true to say that the majority of the successful escapes were accomplished by men but it would be wrong to believe that women only played a minor role in the phenomenon of the escape by Irish political prisoners. Many women had a crucial part to play in the planning, some in harbouring and others as envoys during escapes. One notable escape incident in Mountjoy, which has been well recorded, was the escape of four women from the prison in 1920. Most of what has been written about this particular escape was recorded first hand by Linda Kearns, around whom the escape was centred. She had been captured with three other IRA members while out on an operation near Sligo. So began her sojourn at the pleasure of His Majesty, King George V. Her stay in Sligo Gaol ended when she was transferred to Derry Jail. After Derry it was Armagh and from there she was transferred, 'destination unknown.' Her new destination was Walton Jail in Liverpool. This last transfer seriously interrupted plans which the IRA had to spring her from Armagh Jail. Her recollections of Walton etched a terrible memory in her mind which remained with her al l her life. After a short spell in Walton, she was spirited back to Mountjoy. Kearns' desire for freedom was so great that from the moment she entered Mountjoy she analysed every opportunity to escape. It wasn't long before she was making impressions of the master key after smuggling in dental wax. In the end after a lot of planning and subterfuge she found that the keys did not fit. The women eventually used the oldest method in the book - they went over the wall. Linda recounted the vigorous training they engaged in while the warders looked on in bemusement. Little did they know, but their bemusement and indifference were carefully noted by the political prisoners. The warders soon settled down to a complacent routine in the belief that while the women were behaving like boisterous children they could laze around without being constantly on their guard. On Sunday, 30 October 1920, while the women were playing a football match, their guards retired to the background. The players made plenty of noise, cheering and shouting. One by one the four women slipped away. At a prearranged spot the rope was thrown over the wall. The timing had to be precise to avoid being spotted by the patrol which toured the perimeter wall at regular intervals. All four women scrambled to safety. The four were Linda Kearns, Eileen Keogh, Kathleen Burke and Eithne Coyle. The IRA soon had them in safe billets in and around Dublin. Linda Kearns wrote,

> *Once outside the grey walls of the prison ... we drifted away in the kindly gloom, and we could only clasp each other's hands and whisper again and yet again: 'Is it true? Are we really free?'*

One thing that helped tremendously was the cooperation of the other girls who were left behind. They ensured that the match continued and that the warders did not discover the escape until it was too late.

Two people who later went on to prominence in the Provisional IRA escaped from the Curragh on Wednesday, 24 September 1958. They were Ruari ÓBrádaigh and David O'Connell. Their plan entailed taking a blanket from the hut where the men lived and placing it in the corner of the playing pitches they covered it with grass. During a football match the two men slipped under it and remained concealed until darkness fell. Dummies had been left under the bedclothes which fooled the guards doing the nightly head count. When they thought it was safe enough to come out they cut through the wire and made their escape. They were not noticed missing until 7.30am the following morning. The search of fields around the Curragh lasted for forty-eight hours as the guards, in despair, believed that both men had had too long of a head start.

At Christmas 1971, a Belfast record company could not keep up with the demand for the latest ballad celebrating a group of men dubbed 'the Crumlin Kangaroos.' Their escapades at Belfast Prison made prison security chiefs in the North the butt of many jokes and the laughing stock of Republican community throughout Ireland.

In Crumlin Road Jail
the prisoners one day
A game of football they did have
but the rules did not obey
With the warders watching closely
the passing of the ball

One of the bloody football teams
went up and over the wall

Well its here and up your Arsenal
and a Geordie Best to you
There's not a team in the whole wide world
like the Crumlin Kangaroos

The escape plan involving a football team at Belfast Prison on 16 November 1971, proved to be by far the most sensational escape in the history of the State at that time. The plan was drawn up to include help from outside the prison and after communicating with the prisoners and finalising plans, the escape and rescue operation was set in motion. At 11.10am, during the second half of a football match, rope ladders were thrown over the wall from the Cliftonpark Avenue side of the prison. Before anyone knew what was happening (anyone who was not in on the plan that is) nine men had climbed over the wall. A wire fence had been cut on the pretence of effecting repair and maintenance work. This fence lay between the street and the perimeter wall.

At Stormont, later that day, the Prime Minister for Northern Ireland, Brian Faulkner made an embarrassed report to the Parliament where he claimed that twenty-six prisoners were out on the pitch that day and only for the quick thinking of the warders who ran and pulled one of the ropes off the wall, then the rest of the men would have escaped. He claimed that three warders were attacked by the prisoners and one had to be removed to hospital to be treated for his injuries. During questions in the Stormont Parliament, Brian Faulkner, said the escape was only made possible by the amount of outside assistance given. Additional measures had been taken to improve both the internal and external security and further steps were under further consideration. During the debate Captain Robert Mitchell asked the Prime Minister if he would consider putting electric wire around the jail to "ensure that people who escaped did not escape unharmed."

Mr John Taylor, addressing the Parliament said,
> There will be, of course, a full investigation into how this was allowed to happen. I can only hope that out of today's unhappy events security arrangements will, where necessary, be improved to ensure that this cannot happen again.

He was proved wrong several days later when another three jumped the wall.

One of those 'Crumlin Kangaroos', Terence Clarke, explained how the exercise facilities at the prison especially the use of a football pitch, which had been strategically placed beside the perimeter wall, proved to be too much of a temptation.

"The pitch was built on what used to be called 'the garden' but because of the influx of prisoners into 'the Crum', they needed recreational facilities, especially for internees. Prior to internment there had been renovations at the jail specifically for CT prisoners (Corrective training), Special detention prisoners and YPs (young prisoners who are under 21years). The all weather pitch was specifically for them. They had done away with most of 'the garden' to do that, but because the area of space required for a football pitch, it meant that the pitch was as close to the perimeter wall as you could get, with the exception of what was called 'the scrapyard'.

"At the time there was a campaign to achieve political status between Republicans and Loyalists at 'the Crum'. A self-imposed segregation existed in which all the prisoners were divided into two distinct blocs — one Nationalist and the other what could be termed Unionist. On the day of the escape all the Nationalists were out on the pitch playing football. There were men out on the pitch that day who were in for ordinary civil crimes but the majority of the prisoners in 'the Crum' were Republicans. Certain individuals who were facing, possibly very long sentences before the British courts stayed behind to ensure that the escape was successful.

"The screws tried their best to prevent the escape but they just could not do it because of the determination of the prisoners and also the fact that there were too many of us. There was a fence around the perimeter wall on the outside of the jail. The people on the outside cut that fence and then approached the jail wall to throw the rope ladders over. They then secured those rope ladders and co-ordinated the whole escape from that point. Transport to ferry everyone away from the scene was waiting in a nearby street. It was the original intention to completely empty the football pitch of Republicans. The only thing that prevented this grand plan from working was our (the escapees) inexperience or inability of climbing the face of a wall by rope ladder. Only for that fact, I am sure that many more would have escaped that day. There was certainly enough planning and provision on the outside for such an eventuality. As it was, nine of us got away.

"We were faced with a mad scramble on the actual day. There were people there who did not know what was happening until the rest started running towards the ropes. Obviously in a situation like that you can't ask people to form an orderly queue and ensure that everyone who was going went over the wall in alphabetical order or anything. The Republicans who wanted to get out, knew that they were getting out that day and they knew to expect the signal to run for the ropes once it came.

"On the day we 'went over' there were people outside telling us which cars to get into and as you might guess speed was of the essence, so I would say that we weren't consciously aware of where any particular person was going. I was directed into a car, told to get down, get my football rig off and put on the clothes that had been left in the back. Some of the clothes were too big, others too small, but they did the job. The drivers took us to safe areas where we waited until it was deemed safe to transfer us to a safe house. The safe house was in a well known Loyalist area where, it was believed, the RUC or the Brits wouldn't think of looking for us. Obviously even there, we had to be careful. Although the family looked after us and made us very welcome we would sometimes have to go upstairs or into another room when visitors would call. After seven days at the safe house we were then brought over the border where seven of us appeared at a press conference at Sinn Féin's Dublin headquarters at Kevin Street two days later."

All nine men were from Belfast. Five of them lived within yards of the jail itself — they were, Bernard Elliman, Eugene Fanning and Seamus Storey from the Bone, Terence 'Cleaky' Clarke and Danny Mullan from Ardoyne, Christopher Keenan from Short Strand, Peter Hennessy from the Lower Falls, Thomas Kane from Whiterock and Thomas Fox from Ladybrook.

The RUC and British Army set up security checkpoints all around the jail following the escape and all the usual procedures of checking the ferry terminals and airports were implemented. A careful watch was also kept on those travelling across the border. On November 18th a car was stopped at the border near Omagh. Four men dressed as monks were in the car but on further examination the police realised they had caught two of the escapees, Danny Mullan and Christopher Keenan. All four men were arrested and the two Cistercian monks and the two escapees, along with two other local men appeared in court in connection with the breakout.

The next escape plan involving the distraction of a football match, took place at Long Kesh in 1974. Terence Clarke, who by this time had been recaptured, was again involved, along with several other men from Cage 17. Several plans for escape had been put forward for ratification but were rejected. Eventually, one plan was given the blessing of both the staff inside the prison and the IRA leadership, outside the prison camp.

At Long Kesh, there were two football pitches situated in the centre of the camp. All around the pitches were a total of twenty-two cages. Between the two pitches was a gymnasium and to the side of one of the pitches was what were called 'education huts'. There were also 'single man standing huts' where a warder on the pitch could stand while supervising the prisoners. That meant that there were warders right round the pitch. Inside the gymnasium there were two warders on duty. Unlike 'the Crum', the proximity of a safe haven which was within walking distance of the prison itself was not a reality. Long Kesh was situated next to an British Army camp just outside Lisburn and the surrounding area was regarded as hostile by Republicans The prisoners had by this stage built up a fairly comprehensive plan of the prison layout. After successive escape attempts had reached various stages within the prison complex, the military base and the lanes, roadways and hamlets beyond, the escape committees were clearly aware of where the danger lay. They knew that once they were inside the military base they could 'disappear' quite easily. That was the goal.

The planners set to work and, armed with the wealth of information they had gleaned from successive escapes, they planned to escape by getting through the internee visiting area and going out through the military camp. When the plan was in its final stages, it was submitted to the IRA at Belfast to finalise, and after several modifications the operation was given the green light. Once again the escape was to have taken place during a football match. This time the match was at the all weather pitch in the middle of Long Kesh. Several warders were on duty that day. One of them was actually doing referee. The plan involved taking these warders hostage and tying them up. All the warders would then be held in the gymnasium, which was between the pitches and was isolated from the scrutiny of the other warders in the camp. Prison officers' uniforms would then be used by those escaping. The plan was to go out through the internee visiting area disguised as warders accompanying a visitor. Visiting passes had been forged and everything was in place on the day designated. According to one of the men who was subsequently charged with involvement in this particular escape bid, the breakout was discovered after a PO (a Principle Officer), allegedly, noticed one of the prisoners going past Cage 6.

Once this happened a warder called one of the men over to the wire fence which surrounded the pitch and told him that the escape attempt had been foiled. Unbelievably, the gates from the football pitch right back to Cage 17 had been left open and so the rest of the prisoners who were out on the pitch that day were able to run back into the cage and mingle with the rest of the prisoners there, confusing the head-count. Through actions like this it was hoped that an escapee might have that extra couple of minutes of a head start before the RUC or British Army would know who they were looking for. Six prisoners were eventually charged in relation to this escape attempt. The prison authorities thought they had caught all the main instigators of the plan. What happened next however made them think twice about rejoicing. Once the six men were brought to court, they successfully broke free. With every escape and escape attempt, a dossier of the procedures, layout and reactions were carefully noted so that any future escapes would have a better chance of success.

Portlaoise Prison witnessed several spectacular escapes.

Barbed wire and razor wire have become synonymous with political prisoners.

11. Wirecutters.

The commencement of the Border Campaign in 1956 was greeted with the introduction of internment, North and South of the border. In the South, the internees were held both at Mountjoy and the Curragh Camp. The camp opened in July 1957 and although internment only lasted two years the prisoners tried to escape on several occasions.

The Curragh Camp comprised of wooden huts surrounded with a series of wire fences and ditches. These ditches were six feet deep and eight feet wide. Observation towers were situated at each of the four corners of the camp and were manned night and day by armed Free State soldiers. There was a 'no escape' policy unofficially implemented by the camp staff. This policy led to a split among the internees. The leadership maintained their stance, believing that internment would soon finish and that releases were inevitable before long. They also thought that there was a good chance of being shot dead by the Free State soldiers who guarded the camp, should any escape be attempted. Resentment began to grow within the camp and before long some of the men were planing to disregard the camp staff's directives about escaping. Their plans and disobedience culminated in the successful escape from the Curragh on 3 December 1958.

There were one hundred and sixty-three men interned at the Curragh and in the week prior to the escape the numbers had grown when the twenty two men who had been held at Mountjoy and who had desperately attempted to escape from that building were transferred to here.

A statement of events was issued by the Department for Defence by its Government Information Bureau.

> An attempted mass breakout took place this afternoon amongst some sixty detainees at the Curragh Camp. Sixteen of the detainees made their escape, but one of these was subsequently recaptured.

*Five shots were fired by military guards on duty at the detention
camp over the heads of the group of detainees who were attempting
to escape. Tear gas grenades were also used, as a result of which
two detainees received minor injuries in the legs.
An intensive search is being carried out by Gardaí and military.*

The fact that sixteen men had cut through the wire and made a run for it, left egg
on the face of the government at that time. Not only had sixteen escaped but they
had done so in broad daylight. That afternoon at around 3.45pm, six internees
overpowered the officer in charge of the guards inside the camp. Meanwhile, some
other men quickly cut their way through the wire. It was a desperate move by any
standards which nearly resulted in the death of many of those escaping. Ammonia
grenades exploded between the wires as the men scrambled to freedom. One man
had been shot through the hand as he made good his escape across the trenches and
through the fences. The internees were aided by fog which fell immediately after
the getaway and thereby hampered the search operation by around four hundred
troops.

Those who got away were; J Conlon and William Fagan (Armagh), Joseph
Cunningham (Enniscorthy), M Keogh (Wexford), J Shiels (Navan), T Ferris
(Armagh), Jimmy Devereux (Limerick), Terry O'Toole (Portarlington), Willy
Gleeson (Limerick), P O'Shea (Dublin), J McGirl (Leitrim), D Donaghy (Down),
J McQuaid (Armagh), J Haughey (Lurgan), Norman Day (Lifford) and J Thompson
(Armagh). Of the sixteen who escaped eleven were recaptured and brought back
to the camp. The five who evaded capture, O'Toole, Gleeson, Devereux, Haughey
and Donaghy, made it to the safety of a house at Moon. They had been hunted down
for four days by this stage and one of them, O'Toole, had been shot in the leg.
Internment in the South was phased out and the last of the internees was released
there on 11 March 1959.

The ramifications of this particular escape were to have a reverberating effect
through the ranks of Republican prisoners throughout the country. The 'Border
Campaign' soon lost its momentum and prisoners were gradually released. The
last of the prisoners walked free from 'the Crum' in 1964 before political violence
re-erupted across the North. In 1971 internment was introduced yet again in the
North and internment camps opened. The first and best known of these camps was
Long Kesh, situated just outside Lisburn. The disagreements which existed at the
Curragh, several years previous to this were still smouldering among Republicans
at Long Kesh. In the early days, many of the older Republicans assumed command
of the camp. The internees included a mixture of people, each holding their own
beliefs and loyalties. Among them were members of the Provisional IRA and the
Official IRA but there were also Communists, Socialists, Anarchists and ordinary

Nationalist civilians.

As well as the different political beliefs of the internees there was also the inevitable mixture of personalities. This mixture was volatile at times and meant that young men, full of vigour and daring were constantly vying with older men, set in their ways and much more eager to sit it out. There were others, who, when they weighed up the pros and cons of escaping, chose to stay. After all, they could get released at any time but if caught could face a sentence of up to three years' imprisonment, or even be killed. Internment was a soul destroying process as men waited on tenterhooks anticipating their release. The nature of the Special Powers Act meant that internment could be an indefinite process. For some this was their first experience of imprisonment, let alone imprisonment without trial, but among them were people who had experienced it all before. It therefore took some time before the camp and its inhabitants could settle down into some kind of organised routine.

The camp staff had to assume responsibility for the safety of the prisoners, taking into account what the effect of reprisals would be on the rest of the prisoners. They also had to take into consideration the splits and bad feeling which would have ensued among those not picked to go. Also if an escape went from one side of the camp and was a failure, then the staff had to take on board the subsequent demoralisation throughout the camp. The internees themselves were known as 'The men behind the wire.' It was obvious that before long the prisoners would cut through this barrier and make a run for it. The first men to attempt to cut through the wire were, Billy "Blue" Kelly, Alex Maskey and Geordie Burt. All three men were being held in Cage 4 when they did this. There were eighty-six men in the cage at the time. Going through the wire was the most obvious route out of the camp following in the footsteps of those who left the Curragh in 1958. Their escape did not take place until March 1973. Alex Maskey describes how he escaped that night;

"I had been interned shortly after internment began in 1971. Throughout that period, many men went to the staff with escape plans but they were not allowed to go ahead. There was never any permission given. I was released the following July but I was rearrested soon afterwards and interned once again. My attitude, the second time around, had changed. I knew that I was probably going to be held there until internment ended.

"Internment brings its own frame of mind because there is always the chance of being released early. Many were therefore disinclined to escape but my own view was that I was going to be held in Long Kesh until the end of internment and so I did my utmost to get out. Many people had played around with the idea that the most effective way to get away would be to cut through the wire. On top of that I thought about what I could see, because when we got up on top of the huts we could see out over them, we could see what lay out there between 'no-man's land' and the motorway. We were sure that we could make it but we weren't sure of what exactly we had to face but we knew the risks were there. We knew that the Brits were in the sentry posts. We knew they were armed and we believed that if anybody had been spotted trying to escape they would have been shot. Certainly realising the history of escapes we knew that it had happened before. There was also the danger of being caught and sentenced and prolonging then the time you spent in jail. The primary fact for us was that we needed to try and work out what obstacles were actually facing us. We knew that there were fences. We were told earlier on that there was crisscrossed wire forming a kind of trip wire which would set off flares, across the open ground outside the camp. There were some really negative people who maintained that if you stepped outside the fence you'd be mowed down and that the trip wires were connected to mines which would explode if activated. That these things were used by the British in Palestine and places like that. In my opinion, I think we created more obstacles than were really there.

"Some of the homework prior to the escape was pretty basic. We were able to take all the usual precautions that you would expect to take while doing surveillance work — measurements and times of patrols etc. We also managed to take samples of the razor wire. This wire was lethal. It wasn't like ordinary barbed wire because it sprung and even when you were cutting it, it made a loud report like a shot. It was very dangerous, not only because it could wrap but also because it created a lot of noise. That noise travelling on the cold night air could mean capture or death.

"We knew we would have had to crawl through a series of coils of this wire. We found that a jacket, which in those days was called 'a bomber jacket' was the best coat to have worn through this obstacle. When the razor wire cut it we found that it came back out again without actually penetrating into your skin and snarling you up in the wire. If it stuck in your jeans, for example, it was harder to get it out of them than it was to get it out from one of these bomber jackets. We pointed this out later on when Adams and several others were planning an escape. They had cut the old green shaggy towels to be used as a type of camouflage and we advised them that they would get snarled up in the wire wearing such material. Bomber jackets were, therefore, ideal.

"When we eventually gave our plan to the staff, which by that time was a new staff, we put our plan across quite forcefully. We said that if it was given the go ahead then we would chose the right occasion for the three of us to go. We tried to make an arrangement for transport to pick us up but in the end we settled on a decision to just go on a bad wintry night. Before long the occasion came and we made the bid.

"We arranged to have money in our pockets and obviously cutters and clothes for camouflage. We waited and got the right night to go and we went out. It was, I thought, relatively easy. Our greatest obstacle, we believed would be climbing over the fence on which the observation posts were sited. We thought the blind spot at the observation post was directly underneath the post itself and we made for that spot. This is where the prison designers made their biggest mistake. These observation posts were ultimately designed to thwart any rescue attempts from without rather than a breakout from within. The clean side of the wooden fence was on the outside and the rakes and stays holding the fence in position were on our side of the fence. We were helped to a great degree by this simple factor and we were able to climb up onto these rakes and stays to where the wire was. I still suspect to this day that there was nobody in that post.

We got through onto the open ground and penetrated the crisscrossed trip wire. We had to step over this and, of course, at the same time keep low. We could not talk or make any noise so we were pointing and indicating to one another. It was a bad night, cold and wet and when we cut through the razor wire I was sure that the noise of it could be heard all over the camp. I was waiting to hear the guard dogs barking or see spotlights shining down on us at any minute but we were lucky. We eventually made it across the open ground through the trip wires and through some other fences. The motorway was straight in front of us.

"We heard a Brit patrol coming along and tried to lie low but at this stage we were at the very last fence. The dog came straight over to us. We had said to Blue Kelly to go on ahead and we would hold the attention of the Brits to give him enough time to get away. The Brits panicked once they discovered us. They held us at gunpoint and when they radioed through for help they reported us as intruders. At that stage they did not think there had been a breakout. We began arguing with the Brits while Blue made off. After a while Landrovers arrived on the scene and we were arrested. As we were being brought round, we had to drive by the social club, which was at the jail for the benefit of the warders. The warders were beginning to come out to conduct the head counts. They brought us to the cell block to find out who we were. They identified us but when they went to search the cages, the other internees made their job extremely awkward, and confused the count. The screws had gone in to count everyone, hut by hut, but some people climbed through a window into one hut and then into another so that they did not know how many had got away.

"Blue Kelly, meantime, had got through the last wire fence but had by this stage lost his bearings He started walking and found himself in front of the local police barracks. Realising his mistake he high tailed it back in the other direction. He thumbed a lift from a UDR courier in a van. He spun him a story about his truck having broke down and needing a lift into Belfast to get his partner to come out and tow the truck. The UDR man drove him into the city and dropped him off at Shaftesbury Square. Needless to say there was a lot of bantering after that between ourselves and the Brits because we were saying that it was the Brits who were bringing us into 'the Kesh' and it was the UDR bringing us out.

"Reprisals for the escape were severe. Myself and Geordie Burt were systematically beaten directly after the bid but at least Blue got a good head start. Others were beaten also and the reprisals became an anticipated reaction to all escapes."

Barbed wire or razor wire has become synonymous with prisoners all over the world. It has been used to symbolise the plight of prisoners since its invention. The coils of wire however were deployed quite effectively to securely hold prisoners in captivity.

In March 1973, wire cutters would have come in handy if they had had them at Armagh jail. Armagh had its first jailhouse in 1780. It was situated on the site of a cavalry barracks at Market Street. A new prison at the Mall replaced that old jail and once the jail in Omagh closed in 1881 Armagh became a predominantly women's prison. Not all the escapes and planned escapes involved solely male political prisoners and throughout the history of Ireland women played an invaluable role in the success of escapes. The escape from Armagh jail in 1973, involved five women Tish Holland, Liz McKee and Evelyn Brady from Belfast, along with Marie Maguire and Catherine Robson from Derry.

There were three categories of prisoner being held at the jail; sentenced prisoners, remand prisoners and internees (or detainees as they were later called). Most of those who were being held at the jail had at one time or another visited relatives there on previous occasions and knew the general outlay of the town and the outlay of the prison itself. The British Army were stretched to their limit by 1973 and a detachment of troops was stationed at the prison to guard the prisoners. Inside the jail the women, who had been watching the observation tower, realised that it was empty. It was clear to them that to escape it would only be a matter of getting out through the cell windows and climbing along the walls into that post and from there getting down to the path below. The plans were submitted to the IRA staff at the jail and after some discussion with those outside the jail, the plan was given the green light.

The night picked to go was Wednesday, 4 March. That day on the other landing, Tish Holland and Liz McKee had rearranged the furniture in their cell in the knowledge that it would confuse the warder doing the nightly check and obstruct her view of the cell. They had smuggled in hacksaw blades and had removed the ventilation covers around the windows to saw through the bars. Using ropes which they had previously plaited with wool, they lowered themselves from their windows onto the protective wire screen of the laundry basement and crossed over it to the army observation post. Silence was extremely important because any sound travelled through the still night air.

Maguire, Robson and Brady cut their bars also and all five crossed the walls to the observation post which overlooked the exercise yard. The time was shortly after midnight. The girls could see their transport sitting waiting for them out on the Mall. They could not believe that it could be so easy to get away. Tish Holland was the first to get down onto the wall. She had to get through the razor wire in order to get to the ground below. However the moment she stepped out onto it, it completely enveloped her. Try as the the girls did they could not free her. The Derry girls were to have smuggled in wirecutters but they had been let down at the last minute. Time began to pass as they worked desperately to free Holland but to no avail. The more they pulled and tugged at the wire the more entangled she became. They realised that they were going to be caught.

Inside the prison one of the warders was doing a routine check of the cells. She noticed that in one of the cells three women looked as though they were tucked up and sleeping. They were unnaturally too quiet for that time of night and she at once sent for the keys. When she opened the cell door and checked the beds she found three dummies in place of, Brady, Maguire and Robson. She immediately raised the alarm. The siren began to go off, wailing all over the Mall that night. Outside on the wall the girls still could not free Holland.

Inside the prison the warders were running about frantically searching, believing at first that only three prisoners had escaped, but when they discovered that two detainees had also got away their search immediately intensified. By this stage the prison staff were still unaware that all five women were trapped on the wall of the jail and it was only when they came out to the yard that they discovered the plight of the escapees. McKee, Brady, Maguire and Robson were arrested inside the post. Holland had to be freed from the barbed wire entanglements by a British soldier using bolt cutters. They had been trapped out on the walls for over an hour.

Once they were brought back into the jail they were isolated into single cells as a search of the prison began. Liz McKee, who was one of the escapees maintains that had it not been for the presence of the prison governor, who arrived at the jail once he heard of the escape, the military police would have been let loose on the women. As it was, some of the prisoners were injured in reprisals that night and every prisoner had water hoses turned on them after a scuffle broke out during the searches. Liz does not believe that wire cutters would have been sufficient to cut the wire after seeing the amount of work which was involved to free Holland after she was entangled but she did concede that if they had preplanned the technicalities of overcoming the problems they would encounter at the wire, all five would have escaped that night.

At their subsequent court appearance a spokeswoman for all five said,
> As POWs, we have a duty, to ourselves and our country to make a
> bid for freedom.

Judge Conaghan gave them nine months each. No other escapes were sanctioned from the jail pending the repatriation of the Price sisters but this embargo did not stop the women planning and looking for other ways and means of gaining their freedom. Going through the wire was still a tantalising option.

Armagh Prison

12. Down Under.

Tunnelling is a daunting task. Claustrophobia, asthma, phobia of worms or insects, obesity - all are factors which can hamper the tunnel escaper. One of the most famous underground getaway routes ever recorded in Irish prison history was that from the Curragh camps on 9 September 1921. Up to eighty internees got away on that occasion after tunnelling under the wire. Not one of the escapers were recaptured. The full story of the escape was published in the *Freeman's Journal* on 12 September 1921, much to the embarrassment of the British Government. It read;

> *The tunnel through which the men escaped, it was learned, was fifty feet long and about six feet deep, and was barely wide enough to permit a man's body to pass through. It gave exit to another part of the camp which is in the course of preparation and is not occupied.*
>
> *Large coils of barbed wire were thrown out to prevent escapes and the military guards were particularly watchful at that part. But the compound, unlike the other parts of the camp where internees were confined, was not lighted. To reach that particular spot was then the principle difficulty with which they were faced.*
>
> *Boring operations were started three months ago at another part of the camp, but the authorities discovered what was afoot, with the result that much more stringent precautions than hitherto were adopted by the military. The guards were strengthened and a trench, four feet deep, was dug all around the encampment. Barbed wire, already present in great quantity, was further made use of and placed at possible places of escape. In addition, the internees were warned that if they were seen outside their allotted quarters after 9.00pm they were liable to be fired at by the sentries. The prisoner's huts are visited at regular intervals during the*

night.

Under these circumstances it will be realised how daring was the coup.

The work of constructing the tunnel was necessarily slow, those engaged at it having to proceed with the utmost caution and silence. The job commenced about six weeks ago in one of the large huts, each of which contains about twenty-five men. A large hole was dug in the ground floor, and as the tunnel progressed, planks were placed over the cavity while the operation successfully proceeded.

The ground in certain parts was wet and clammy, and a number of props had to be inserted to keep the earth from falling in. In the process of excavation the crudest instruments and tools were used, and throughout the whole of the work the only articles available consisted of a few knives and forks and pieces of old iron which were found lying about the camp.

To conceal the clay and debris was a task which at first baffled all efforts, but the difficulty was at length surmounted.

Excitement, hot but subdued, pervaded the whole body of internees when on Thursday night all arrangements were completed and the moment had arrived to bring their plans to fruition.

Three or four men, specially picked for the occasion, acted as the advance party. Having gone through the narrow cutting they had cut away through the barbed wire entanglements. This involved considerable risk, as the sentry boxes were but a few yards away and the least noise would attract the attention of the guards. The night was calm but it was dark and foggy.

The internees escaped in batches of eight or ten. Getting through the tunnel was so tedious that the time occupied by each man was fully two and a half hours. Each man crawling along, followed on the heels of his comrade.

Occasionally progress was interrupted by some unanticipated occurrence and low whispers went along the line of creeping men. Every man was told to halt and lie quiet until some necessary reconnoitring had been done. Then the signal, "All's well," was given and the crawling process was resumed.

The most dangerous part of the journey was that following the exit from the tunnel. At any moment armed guards with flashlights were liable to pass that way and then the discovery was almost certain. At one time the guard was within two yards of the exit, but he did not look that way.

Throughout the whole night the men continued in an unbroken line *to burrow their way out.*

A large number of those who escaped roamed all over the plains adjoining the camp before they found the trail in the darkness.

Some strayed into the Bog of Allen, whilst others, after walking nearly an hour, found themselves back again in the neighbourhood of the camp.

Begrimed and bedraggled the escaped men presented a strange appearance as they marched in groups through the open country.

Such accounts on the plight of the internees were read with great admiration, the length and breadth of Ireland. Michael Collins was asked for his opinions on the events. Aware that Treaty negotiations were by then in full swing and that a release of over three thousand Irish internees was predicted as the preliminary first step, Collins declared that he was delighted with what had occurred. He declared that, 'the prisoners had, for the first time, escaped without the cooperation from the outside.' It would have been a breech of the Truce had there been any outside cooperation, but it was no breech of the Truce to express delight at their being free again. The next use of a tunnel went out under the walls of Kilkenny Jail ten weeks later. This time forty-four got away, having first taken over eight tons of clay from below ground and scattering it around the disused part of the jail from which they worked.

The escape of the prisoners from Kilkenny jail on 22 November 1921, matched the jail breaking episode of the Curragh. Between 7.00pm and 8.00pm a few passers-by outside the jail were astonished to see the crust of the road breaking and two men emerge from the opening. The men, dishevelled and begrimed, at once became alert. They immediately ordered the dumbfounded witnesses back, shepherding them into batches and after taking over one of a row of cottages nearby, they imprisoned them behind closed doors. They then returned to the hole from which they had emerged and cleared away the obstructing debris.

This done, prisoner after prisoner emerged, all dishevelled and dirty but none lost any time in putting between himself and the prison a long stretch of country. When the last man had come out of the hole, alarm whistles sounded inside the jail. The mass escape had been discovered. Military and police in lorries were soon on the scene and in an incredibly short time the whole countryside was in ferment. Nightfall however lent her aid to the escaping men who took to the fields where the lorries could not follow. The leader of the escapees was called Condon and it was claimed that he was the first man out. He stayed at the tunnel entrance until the last man was safely away. The other prisoners came out of the subterranean passage at intervals. Their progress along the fifty foot long tunnel had been slow and laborious. Some of the prisoners had lighted candles and it is said that a plank was laid along the base of the burrow on which they managed to crawl through. Some were scantily dressed, while others were wearing great coats and were carrying bags as though anticipating a long journey. Three prisoners were inside the tunnel when the alarm was raised, but they were not abandoned, and were helped to safety by their comrades.

An examination of the interior of the prison revealed how the clever coup had been meticulously planned. In the floor of a large cell, where all the prisoners met, a hole had been made leading to the underground cell below. This section of the jail had not been in use for some time, being originally used as punishment cells akin to castle dungeons, and so the prisoners could work away without being disturbed. Through the wall, dividing this cell from another cell, a large aperture had been made. It was in the corner of this cell that the boring of the tunnel commenced. The hole in the floor of the large cell was reported to have been so neatly cut that its detection was virtually impossible. The distance of the tunnel from the prison cell to the exit at the public road was approximately fifty yards and at the point where the prisoners emerged it was reported to have been as deep as eight feet. All the clay which had been dug from the tunnel was sent back along its length and deposited in the cell where the tunnelling began. Every prisoner in that wing of the jail escaped, all of whom had been convicted by court-martial and more than one had been serving a life sentence.

It was with these successes that jail tunnellers began to perfect their trade. Many of the most sensational escapes happened at that time and inevitably prison security advisors tightened the regimes at jails and camps throughout the country to prevent any further development of this *modus operandi*. Extra checks were made by prison guards and extra pill boxes, trenches and fences were erected. Nevertheless tunnelling continued. In the 1940's the most successful tunnel was dug at Derry jail from which twenty-one men made a run for freedom. There were many tunnels which were discovered due to both good observation techniques by the jail authorities and bad security practices by the prisoners themselves. When the North erupted in 1969, the government reintroduced internment under the Special Powers Act. The final consequence of this detention policy was the establishment of an internment camp at Long Kesh, a former RAF base outside Lisburn.

Long Kesh lent itself to tunnelling. Situated on boggy land just outside Lisburn it was opened as an internment camp in September 1971. When the camp first opened to house internees it comprised five compounds which were based roughly along the lines of a prisoner of war concentration camp. Long Kesh operated a similar regime. The prisoners elected their own camp staff and a Commanding Officer negotiated with the commander of the camp's guards. Prisoners were housed in Nissan huts with a shared ablutions facility. By 1974 the camp comprised twenty-two cages, or compounds, and had a population of fifteen hundred internees. Due to the adverse publicity the place received, the authorities tried to rechristen the prison as HMP Maze, but the nomenclature of Long Kesh remained.

Life inside one of these camps was much more open and noisy than life in jail. There was very little privacy with up to sixty men sharing a hut together. At one stage it is said that tunnels were being dug in every cage as men's frustration at being imprisoned without trial away from their homes and families reached new proportions. A fresh round of sectarian murders had began in the North and people both inside and outside the jail were anxious for their safety. These internees had became known internationally as "The men behind the wire."

It wasn't long before the chances of escaping began to become even more possible. In the beginning several people had escaped in ones and twos. Some tried getting out dressed up as priests while others hid inside delivery lorries or bin lorries. On 11 March 1973, Billy Kelly from Belfast's Carrick Hill cut through the wire — the first man ever to do so. The camp staff however had bigger plans in their minds. They planned to burrow beneath the wire and free as many men from Cage 5 as possible. Many problems were encountered on the way. It was winter when the final stages of the plan came together. The winter was a bad time to dig a tunnel due to the flooding but after a revolt by the internees in October, the camp was burned. The following day the women prisoners at Armagh Jail took the governor and three warders hostage. That same evening a riot erupted at 'the Crum' and Magilligan Camp was burned. The British Army, RUC and UDR were all put on full alert as the situation got worse. No one had escaped during all the disturbances as the police and army fought to regain control of the prisons. The British Army immediately set about building Long Kesh back up again with the prisoners *in situ*. This meant that there was rubble lying about which enabled the prisoners to salvage odds and ends for the purpose of shoring up the inside of the tunnel. Right under the noses of warders and armed British soldiers the internees in Cage 5 said their goodbyes and escaped through a carefully constructed tunnel in the floor of Hut 25. The British Army thought Long Kesh was escape-proof. Just in case it wasn't they had an aeroplane fitted with special thermal imaging cameras and up-to-date infra-red surveillance equipment. This plane, an RAF Phantom Jet, had a regular fortnightly flight from an air base in England. The jet flew over the camp taking aerial photographs in an attempt to detect any underground 'disturbances'. The flight landed at RAF Aldergrove to leave off the film to be studied before returning to base. What they did not account for was the internees ingenuity at spotting any weakness in their regime. The charred remains from the fire gave perfect cover to dump the excess soil during excavation and the men took the full advantage of this opportunity. "They were able to dispose of the soil much more easily than would normally be possible," explained an embarrassed prison source. After the camp was burned the regular routine had been temporarily dispensed with and, in the confusion, the escape came to fruition. The debris provided a great opportunity to disperse the surplus soil — the most difficult technicality for the tunnellers to overcome. The entrance to the tunnel was a mere eighteen inches in diameter and a shaft went down five feet at the base of which was the start of a sixty-five yard long tunnel. The length proved to be an engineering nightmare since the materials for shoring up such a tunnel were in very short supply. However, bits of bed iron and pieces of wood were gathered, here, there and everywhere, and a successful tunnel was bored right under the noses of the prison guards. On the night of 5 November 1974, the escape of the prisoners was further aided by the weather. A shroud of mist had settled over the entire area thus hampering those guards in the watch towers and security patrols on the ground from having an unobstructed view of the prison.

The following is a report which appeared in a Republican newspaper the following week, it is a first-hand account by one of the escapees who was later recaptured.

"I was in the first squad to go down the tunnel and out. Gerry went out first. Nipper went second and then I went third. I followed straight behind the first two. I left paper markers behind me. I crossed the road into the trench. I watched for W. coming behind me. At the time of the shooting Gerry, Nipper and I were at the first barbed wire roll in the field between the perimeter fence and the M1. When the shooting occurred I told the two in front of me to lie still, since I did not think we were spotted. We listened to all the commotion behind us. When no lights hit us we crawled on to the next fence. We cut this and went on through and across another road to another roll of barbed wire. We went through that. Gerry had dropped the cutters. After going through this we landed in a water ditch. The whole place by this time was lit up so we went left a bit and into the bank of the ditch. The three of us crept into the hole in the bank which we dug (an hour to an hour and a half after leaving the tunnel). We lay in this dugout until darkness fell on the Wednesday evening, when we pulled out and crawled to the right into a potato field between us and the M1. At the bottom of the potato field we turned right and headed for the pick-up spot. Once there we stayed a while, then made for the the railway line. We followed this past Lisburn and then took to the fields and came out at Dunmurry Lane. We walked up Dunmurry Lane. I suggested taking to the fields again but it was decided against this. We were caught at the bridge at Dunmurry Lane."

Tragedy struck once the sentries realised what was happening. There were many conflicting stories told of what actually happened, but one man, 24 year-old Hugh Coney from Coalisland, was shot dead as he emerged from the tunnel. Many of those captured were brutally beaten by British soldiers. Meanwhile inside the camp the remaining detainees heard the shooting, and, as the army moved in to conduct a head-count, a riot soon developed. CR gas and rubber bullets were fired at the prisoners. Twenty-seven men were treated in the prison hospital while two had to be taken to an outside hospital, as their injuries were more serious. As the casualty figure rose, an emergency telephone service was set up at Hillsborough to take calls from anxious relatives. An uneasy silence reigned in Belfast as thousands of people came out onto the streets of the city in protest at the summary executions of unarmed internees. The maximum sentence for escape at that time was three years.

As rumour gave way to reality, the enormity of the escape was realised. Thirty-one men had escaped but were arrested at the mouth of the tunnel. One had been shot dead and the three who got away, Edward Maguire, Gerard Rice and James Walsh, were arrested at Dunmurry. Morale among the men was at an all time low, as not only were the men in Cage 5 ready to go out that night in batches, but the wire between Cages 4 and 5 had been cut and relays of men from that cage had also been standing by to join them. The others who were later charged with escaping were, Billy Johnston, Frank Johnston, Brian Maguire, Frank McCann, Brendan Shannon, James Walsh, Sean McClorey, John Dornan, John McQuillan, Pat Rice, James Barr, Sean Convery, Joe Barrett, Dennis Brown, Joe Corr, John Dorris, Paddy Fitzsimons, Paddy Holden, Tony Hughes, Michael Mullan, James McErlean, William McAllister, Dominic O'Neill, Francis Rice, Sean Scott, Thomas Taylor and John Francis Walsh.

Undeterred by the outcome of events that November night the prisoners continued tunnelling. It was later revealed that over two hundred tunnels had been discovered at Long Kesh by 1978. Some tunnels, or parts of them, were used again. Other dummy tunnels were dug to put the prison security off the scent. Sometimes the tunnel could be too short and others were too close to the surface, with the result that on many occasions the tunneller would get the unwelcome surprise of a guard falling in on top of him. Then, there were the problems of shoring, air circulation and ventilation, disposing of the excavated soil and encountering large rocks. One of the problems with the tunnels was that the water levels in the winter tended to rise dramatically, rendering any tunnels which had not allowed for this process, flooded.

On Wednesday, 5 May 1976, the local newspapers blazed a headline detailing the successful escape of nine Republican prisoners. They had escaped from Long Kesh earlier that day after crawling along a tunnel, cutting their way through a security fence, and scaling the twenty foot-high perimeter wall. One of the men was later recaptured by the RUC as he and another man made off through fields. All those who escaped were being held in the Irish Republican Socialist Party Cage which was Cage 5 at the time. They included Cahir O'Doherty, Eddy McNicholl, Seamus O'Kane, Harry Flynn, Hen Doherty, Jake McManus, Joe Kelly, Gerry Clancy and Gerard Steenson. The tunnel was just over forty feet long and led from the hut where the prisoners were being held, to just inside the last boundary fence. The entrance of the tunnel had been similar to that which was cut in Kilkenny jail in 1921. The escape began in the early hours. After crawling along, they surfaced close to the fence, which they cut through with wire cutters. They then dashed to the recently built perimeter wall. Here they used ropes made from sheets and blankets, and hooks made from chair legs, to scale it. The remainder of the prisoners in the Cage behaved normally and the guards did not realise that the prisoners had escaped until they unlocked the Cages the following morning. British soldiers from the 4th Royal Tank Regiment immediately put into operation a prearranged plan but it was to no avail. Nine men escaped. Cahir O'Doherty explains how the escape developed;

"We were moved from the top of the camp down to Cage 5. In the Cage there were two big huts and a half hut. Then there was an education hut and a hut where we showered etc., This cage was right beside the perimeter and it meant that not only was it the easiest one to tunnel from but also that it was always under scrutiny by the screws. After the escape in which Hugh Coney was shot dead, the Brits started to build a wall around the camp. We had been looking at different ways of escape prior to the tunnel and one was to cut the wire. We cut it in an L shape, and that way, you could not notice it as it sprang back into place.

"Our cage was beside the wall and we did go out once into 'no man's land', which lay between us and the perimeter wire, but all sorts of things went wrong, which led to us having to try and get back in again without being detected. We eventually started a tunnel. I would say that it probably took between three and four weeks to complete for we had three to four ground searches while the tunnelling was going on. During a ground search the screws would come in and tap the floors of the hut. If it rang hollow then they would discover where the tunnel entrance was. To beat this we began smuggling in cement in little bags until we had enough to make a concrete slab. The entrance was in the floor of the end hut and was concealed and disguised with four floor tiles to resemble the rest of the floor. When in position you would never had known the tunnel was there.

"The tunnel was a huge operation and involved up to thirty men. Some were digging, some sewing, others dispensing with excess soil and the rest doing bits and pieces. Having said that, not everyone was aware of what was happening. We broke through the floor and dug out the shaft of the hole first of all. The Kesh was named after *an ceis fada*, which means 'the long bog' and that is precisely what it was. There was only about six feet of clay and then you were on to a level seam of sand. Below the sand was water and the water finds its own level. We basically had to stay inside the sand and we knew we were going in a straight line. It was pretty basic mathematics after that. We moulded aluminium trays into shovels and began digging.

"To avoid being detected by the Brits' 'eye in the sky' we put all the sand into bags and put the bags into the hole again after a day's work was done. Next day we pulled out all the bags and burrowed a little further. All the surplus sand was emptied in the cavity walls of the Nissan hut where we lived. The most important thing was to ensure that there was no trace of sand left outside the tunnel. When you came back up someone always checked the soles of your shoes. After you showered someone always came behind you and made sure there was no sand left over in the basin.

"Everyone was enthusiastic about success and by the time it came to go we paired off. The pairs always comprised a countryman and a city man. There were several mishaps during the tunnelling. At one stage I remember a man got stuck. Being stuck in a tunnel would be like being buried alive, after all, there is not an awful lot of room down there to manoeuvre. We had to get someone to crawl up and tie a rope around his legs and then we pulled him out.

"Digging the tunnel was fairly easy though because it was sand. The tunnel had to be kept small to prevent it being discovered and to enable us to dispose of the least surplus sand as possible. We also had a way of providing ventilation in the tunnel. We took the heating element out of an extractor fan and then used the fan to pump fresh air into the tunnel. We made a funnel with soup cans. Both ends were cut off to provide us with a tin tube, then we removed the shower curtains. These we cut up to make sleeves, which were sewed to fit around the cans and in this way we had a makeshift ventilation unit. We only used this system part of the way, because after a while we were outside the perimeter fence and we could pierce a hole from below.

"Digging took place during the day rather than at night. We believed that the noise would be detected easier at night than in the day time, when everything else is happening, so we blared the radio and continued with our task. We were down there flat on our stomachs with our arms outstretched in front. To get out we had to wriggle out backwards. During tunnelling we came across concrete. This was the base of the perimeter fence. What had happened was that a tract had been dug out by a digger when the camp was being constructed and the posts were concreted in. To go under this meant that we might be going down into the water but we were okay. It was a good marker for us. Probably the worst thing about the tunnel was the silence. It was literally like being in a grave. It was completely dark. When you close your eyes you think it is dark, well I can tell you, when you're down a tunnel it's what you call, really dark. You cannot see anything at all. You can hear your heart beating. You can also hear the other guy's heart beating in the silence. We had been making good progress and it was our intention to tunnel under the two wire fences and get as close to the perimeter wall as possible. In case there were any hiccups we smuggled in wire cutters and in the hut we put together a makeshift rope ladder complete with rungs. The escape was to have coincided with May Day but in the end it actually took place on 5 May, and even that date was picked because disaster struck at the last moment.

"We had been having particularly wet weather and I remember looking out the window this day and noticing that the ground had caved in. We immediately had a meeting to discuss what to do and it was this eventuality which prompted us to move as quickly as possible. We threw a mattress over the hole in the ground and immediately got down and began to redig around where it had collapsed.

"We went in the early hours of the morning and I was the last man out. There were ten of us altogether and we went out in pairs. The tunnel came up beside the second fence and we cut that and then ran across open ground to the wall. I had the rope ladder but because of the rungs it was too heavy to throw up. The wall was about twenty-two foot high. Anyhow, Harry Flynn pulled over a plank that had been lying on the ground and wedged it up against the wall. He then climbed up the plank and from that position was able to hook the rope over the wall. One of the lads had to return because he couldn't climb the rope and I left him back to the tunnel. When I got back I climbed over the wall and as I was getting down the other side I had a bad fall. We were really lucky that the Brits in the sentry posts did not see us. On the other side of the wall there were reels and reels of razor wire to get through before we could reach the M1 motorway. Just down a bit from where we were standing was another security post and we could see the Brits inside it. We noticed that they had cut a pathway through the reels in order to do patrols with dogs so we used their path to get through this last obstacle course. Once on the road I decided that it would be a bad idea to set off together and so me and Gerard Steenson broke away from the pack and headed for Belfast. We got as far as Sprucefield when I was caught crossing a field. I was arrested and brought to the local barracks but they still did not know who I was. A couple of hours later they got the news of what had happened, by which stage Steenson had also been caught. The rest of the lads got away. I heard later that a car had been driving up and down looking out for us to take us to safe houses but we didn't see it. In the end I got another eighteen months for escaping. The judge said that he felt justified in giving us such a sentence because the only lives we had put in danger were our own."

After this escape the government decided to add other deterrents. The wall had not hampered the escape because the men quite safely scaled it. It was decided to run coils of razor wire along its length. This too was changed when it was realised that the wire, instead of making it more difficult to get over the wall, actually made it easier because now there was something for the hook to catch onto. Once this was realised, the anti-grappling tubes were thought of, and are now a regular feature around every prison throughout the country. The escape committees went back to the drawing board to plan other ways of overcoming these latest developments and before long came up with several alternatives.

The government however were also back at the drawing board. With every escape they were learning. Their development of a new 'super jail' was beginning to take shape, on paper at least.

The 'tank' used by the Dublin IRA in an attempted breakout from Portlaoise on Saint Patrick's Day 1975.

13. Off with a Bang

In the twenty-six counties by the 1980s, Portlaoise and Limerick jails had become the government's top security prisons for the detention of Republican prisoners. Portlaoise had the biggest population of Republicans after all the Republican prisoners at Mountjoy were transferred to that jail in November 1973, following the helicopter escape of the IRA's Chief of Staff. It was only when this happened that the prison began to come into the public eye. Portlaoise Prison was built in 1830 and was extended in 1901. The regime within this prison complex was no easier than the one imposed on Republican prisoners by the British Government. It too, soon became the scene of hunger strikes and riots. What has been significant about Portlaoise prison was that it has featured most prominently in the use of explosives to help the escapee gain his freedom.

The introduction of explosives was by no means a novel idea. The Fenians had played about with the idea with tragic consequences one hundred years earlier. During the civil war explosives were used in Dundalk. On 17 July, 1922, Dundalk was captured by the pro-Treaty forces. The barracks in Anne Street and the jail were both captured and three hundred prisoners were reported to have been taken. Once they had full control of the town, the civilian prisoners at the jail were moved, and their places were taken by Republican prisoners.

A fortnight later, on 27 July, the town was rocked by a huge explosion at the side of the jail wall and it was estimated that one hundred and six political prisoners escaped. Much of what happened that day was subject to severe censorship by the new government authorities but from various news reports of the time we know that two soldiers were shot dead and a woman was seriously injured in the process.

At 7.30am the western end of Dundalk was shaken by a terrific explosion. Every window in the dwelling houses in the vicinity of the prison was smashed by the force of the blast. The County Infirmary which was situated just opposite the prison was also considerably damaged. As a result of the attack a huge hole was blown in the prison through which prisoners escaped. It was said that they were seen to dash through the streets of the town and most made off into the open countryside. Two soldiers, who were shot, died as a result of ambushes designed to attract attention of the pro-Treaty forces away from the jail. There was a great deal of commotion immediately after the explosion as it had been accompanied, simultaneously, by several attacks on the soldiers who were garrisoned at the town at the time. One of the entrances of the barracks (the Quay Street entrance) was blocked by the placing of a railway engine across the gates. The engine had been driven from the adjoining Greenore line and was brought to a halt midway between the gates thus preventing traffic at that point going any further. At the other entrance many shots were fired at the troops passing Barrack Street Bridge.

Several leading IRA men were among the escapees. Thirty men were recaptured within twenty-four hours of their escape. Some had reached Drogheda. Among the most notable of those captured was John McCoy of Mullaghbawn, who held the rank of Brigadier in the military barracks prior to the town being captured by the pro-Treaty forces. Cardinal Logue, the Catholic Primate for the Diocese, in the aftermath of the escape threatened to excommunicate anyone who was involved in the breakout.

Dundalk set the style for subsequent escape attempts. In May 1990 at Belfast Prison, a similar plan was foiled after a bomb was discovered in transit to the perimeter wall. The planners realised that smuggling the explosives into the jail could mean that the prisoners themselves could place the charges wherever they needed them. Smuggling is a trade which has been perfected by inmates in prisons throughout the world and it came as no surprise to the prison staff that explosives would be far easier to smuggle into jail than guns.

In May 1974 the prisoners began to put an escape plan into operation at Portlaoise. Tunnelling began immediately but the following month their plan was uncovered. The discovery of the tunnel, which had been dug to a length of eighty feet, dashed the prisoner's hopes of freedom. On Sunday 18 August 1974 at 12.30pm, nineteen prisoners escaped by blowing a hole in the wall of the prison. A weakness in the jail security was noticed in the laundry area. The laundry led on to an outside stairway that led down to the courtyard. It led to the Governor's House and to the right was the warders mess, where they relaxed whilst off duty. Access to the laundry was not too difficult, as the prisoners quickly realised.

Several men who had been involved in the helicopter escape from Mountjoy found themselves involved in the Portlaoise escape. Gerry O'Hare recalls what happened that day, having only a matter of weeks to serve he was on the top landing of the jail along with Martin McGuinness from Derry chatting about Gaelic football with a senior prison officer.

"The escape committee were already aware that a doorway at the top of the yard led practically on to the streets of Portlaoise. Word was sent outside to those responsible for assisting jail escapes. They quickly sent news back in that the plan looked viable. But how were they to break the door down? Explosives.

"On the Friday before the planned escape a couple of leading Republicans were arrested in the vicinity of the town and brought to Portlaoise. It seemed a bad omen. However, the decision to proceed was made and a tense Saturday into Sunday took place. A party of six men were chosen as the first group to make the break. A back-up team of six were chosen to follow, and after that it was a case of every man for himself.

"During the previous weeks the prisoners had spent their time making screws' uniforms, shirts and hats. It was felt that in the rush for the gate, the soldiers on the roof would be unsure of who was chasing who, and could therefore not afford to open fire. This is precisely what happened.

"Sunday lunchtime arrived but nobody could eat. The tension was unbearable. Chatting to the screw, Martin and myself kept our eyes on the lower landing. Liam Brown approached the screw, asked to be let in and he duly obliged. As he opened the door the first team who were placed in cells nearby rushed forward as Liam grabbed the laundry key from the startled screw. Quickly overpowered by the prisoners, he could see clearly that resistance was futile. The prisoners opened the door and quickly descended the stairway, followed almost immediately by the second group and about twenty-five others. As they raced to the top of the yard, the soldiers panicked allowing those vital seconds for the first group to place the explosive device on the door.

"The resulting explosion was deafening for such a small device but it opened the door. As the first of the prisoners rushed out of sight the soldiers on the roof opened fire above the heads of those following. Quite wisely, those who were at the rear realised the game was up and dropped to the ground. Screws rushed from their mess in a state of shock and I remember one shout in a panic, 'Don't shoot, don't shoot'. The soldiers recognised him and the shooting stopped.

"Those who failed to make the break were brought back in to the prison and the Governor arrived shortly afterwards and demanded a head-count. This was refused and we milled around for several hours refusing to go to our cells thus causing the utmost confusion. Only after several hours and under the threat of a riot did the OC order us to stand by our cells. We had been doing our own head-count and thought the number of escapees to be about fourteen. Imagine the cheer that went up when the Governor was heard to groan 'Nineteen, f***ing nineteen.' A veteran screw of the helicopter escape came up to me later, and with a smile said, 'Nobody was hurt. None of your men or mine and that's all that matters."

About half of those who escaped that day were from the North. As a result of the escape, one of the South's biggest ever search operations went into action. Roadblocks were set up immediately and the systematic search of all of County Wexford began. Every outhouse and building was searched. The Navy were also put on the alert. The searches continued for over a fortnight. By the Saturday Police spokespersons were confident of catching all those who escaped but all was in vain. The prisoners had got away. Back at the prison the Government decided to ban all incoming food parcels saying that 'the risk involved was no longer regarded as being acceptable' as they believed that the explosives were smuggled inside a box of sweets.

The nineteen who escaped were: Liam Brown, Paddy Devenny and Micky Nolan from Belfast, Francis McFeely and Ian Milne from Derry, Thomas McGinty and Eddie Gallagher from Donegal, Patrick Thornberry, Kevin McAllister and Martin McAllister from Armagh, Francis Hughes and Kevin Mallon from Tyrone, Oliver McKiernan from Fermanagh, Bernard Hegarty and Sam O'Hare from Louth, Michael Kinsella, Sean Kinsella from Monaghan, Sean Morris from Meath, and Anthony Weldon from Dublin.

> The Army shouted 'Blast it', I took the gelignite
> The Governor shouted 'Blast it', I set the fuse alight
> Then Mallon shouted 'Blast it', so I did with all my might
> To the border to the border we'll be heading for tonight
>
> On the eighteenth day of August, in Portlaoise Prison yard
> While we went out for exercise, the army stood on guard
> The warders watched us closely
> For suspicions to be seen
> Well they watched and watched for one of us
> and missed the brave nineteen.

An inquiry was held into security arrangements at the prison. This was conducted by Mr Justice Finlay who made several recommendations, namely that the position of Director of Security should be established. That person's remit would be to coordinate the activities of both the police and army who have responsibility for security at Portlaoise.

In that December of 1974, at Portlaoise, following many of the subsequent 'security restrictions' one hundred and twenty prisoners took twenty-seven prison warders hostage in a seven hour takeover of 'E' Wing at the jail. The revolt was the culmination of many protests by the prisoners who believed that many of the rights that they had won after a twenty-one day hunger strike in September / October 1973 had been denied to them as part of the government's response to the 'Provie Birdie' escape. The riot which was suppressed by a contingent of two hundred armed soldiers and guards was followed by a hunger strike. On 4 January 1975, ten PIRA members embarked on a hunger strike for the improvement of conditions at the prison. Ten days later another six men joined the fast. After protracted negotiations and with one of the hunger strikers close to death the strike was called off after its forty-fifth day. On 6 February, the press were reporting that explosives had been found hidden in a cavity in a cell wall during a routine search. Saws, chisels, knives, gate keys and ropes were also found. At the end of the hunger strike Portlaoise staff and prison security advisors had believed that women visitors to the jail had been smuggling explosives into the prison after they arrested a Belfast woman passing over explosives to a visitor. As a result visits were suspended for a fortnight. They were resumed on 11 March. Eventually amidst all this turmoil it became evident that the escape committee had been busy planning the next move. Less than a week later on Saint Patrick's Day 1975 the prison was to witness what could have been another successful break for freedom. Unfortunately, one man died, as yet again explosives were used to breach the prison security. Crucial questions remained unanswered as to who fired the shots, as the Irish Army, who were on guard that night, maintained that they came under sniper fire. It was believed that the key to the escape was a specially adapted lorry which was to be used to break through the gates. This vehicle, a four wheel drive gravel dumper, had been fitted with half-inch thick steel plates which virtually converted the machine into a gigantic tank. On the front of the machine was a steel battering ram. The windows were sheeted with steel with just a slit for the driver to look through. Even the wheels were protected with steel guards. It had been painted camouflage green and was driven into position at around 8.30pm that night. It smashed through the gates of the prison farmyard and drove towards the perimeter wire thirty or forty feet from the walls. It was here that it was believed that the mistake occurred. Instead of turning and smashing through the side gate of the prison the 'tank' went along the perimeter wall and got bogged down in mud. The electricity surrounding the jail was cut off. The rescuing party had thrown a chain across an ESB transformer nearby but the prison's security lights remained on. Just at that moment there were two loud explosions. One at the doorway of the recreation hall and the other at a wire perimeter. These explosions enabled the prisoners to gain access to yet another outer compound. They were still inside the prison walls. The shooting lasted for more than a half hour and as a result of the controversy over who fired first the government released a statement explaining what had happened:

> *After the first explosion some shots were fired by the military, the result of which was that there was one fatality and two injuries, one a suspected thigh injury, the other a suspected hand injury. All of the casualties were prisoners and the two injured were removed to the military hospital at the Curragh.*
>
> *At about the same time as the other incidents began, a lorry was crashed through the farm gate from the Dublin Road and was driven down the farm road towards the prison compound. It stopped some distance from the compound but close to it.*
>
> *A number of men - believed to be four - were seen running from the lorry and two men are now helping Gardaí with their inquiries in relation to this incident.*

No prisoners escaped on this occasion. The man who was shot dead that night was Thomas Smyth, an IRA volunteer.

After this incident the prison authorities banned parcels of every description amid vociferous protest from the prisoners. In August 1976, five men blasted their way out of the basement of the Special Criminal Court at Green Street in Dublin. Four men were recaptured almost immediately but one man, Michael O'Rourke made it to the USA. The government decided to declare a State of Emergency. Using the Offences Against the State Act, new legislation was drawn up under the emergency powers bill. It was proposed that the length of time an IRA suspect could be held before being charged should be lengthened. The sentence for IRA membership was risen from two to seven years. Additional powers of search and arrest were conferred on the Army and under the Criminal Law Bill new procedures were brought into force to control the press and media.

The IRA has resorted to the use of explosives on many other occasions. Learning from the failure of the Fenians at London, the Republicans went on to perfect their bombing technique. It was with such a background, and with the advancement of newer and more effective weaponry, that the IRA began to use explosives to blow down the walls of their prisons. Escaping is a high risk operation and as prison security procedures developed so did the escape committee's ideas. In 1977 the IRA agreed to smuggle explosives into Belfast Jail in order to effect the biggest escape ever seen in the city. The escape would allegedly have been based on a similar operational plan used in London, Dundalk and finally Portlaoise. The plan was discovered before it could be put into motion.

Unknown to the prison authorities the Republicans had been receiving gelignite hidden inside butter in their food parcels. Before long a sizeable amount of gelignite had been amassed to blow down all the internal gates and doors leading to the perimeter wall. Outside help was believed to also be planning to blow a hole in the perimeter walls. The plot failed after an explosion in a cell in 'C' Wing (the result of a Loyalist bid to gain segregation from the Republican prisoners) led to an order to 'dump arms.' A search of the prison yards later revealed packets of gelignite which were said to have been thrown from the cell windows. It was reported that had the prisoners successfully carried out their plans they could have made the prisons walls fall like those of Jericho. The impact, had the plan succeeded, can only be guessed. This basic plan was attempted again in the late 1980s but the plan was abandoned after it was realised that the RUC had been tipped off by an informer. On 7 October 1989, the RUC and British army moved in to the area and upon searching a mechanical digger which had been parked alongside the perimeter wall of the prison, they discovered a 750lb bomb placed in the front bucket of the vehicle. In the subsequent search inside the jail 6lbs of semtex, a revolver and ammunition were discovered. The prison security authorities later stated that they believed that the explosives, or the weapon, had been smuggled in inside the hollowed out heel of a training shoe. They sent a memo throughout the other British prisons advising them to be on the alert. The only time that explosives have been used with success in the 1970s was at Portlaoise prison. Any further attempts to reenact these plans at a later date, failed.

On Sunday 24 November 1984 there was an attempted escape of twelve Republican prisoners from Portlaoise. Most of the other prisoners were attending Mass in E3 Wing. Back on the landing the warder was held at gunpoint by one of the prisoners. The escapees wore warders' uniforms under their coats and they made off out of the main prison building using duplicate keys. There were seven gates in all to pass through. The last obstacle was a steel door which the prisoners intended to use explosives to blast through. A charge was set against the door but the explosion only buckled it. Trapped inside this last section all the men surrendered. They each received three years for attempting to escape.

British soldier on guard outside The Maze Cellular after the mass escape of September 1983.

14. Across the Water

Escapes from prisons in Britain by Irish prisoners has been a regular feature in the turbulent history of Britain's Irish War. Prison struggles in Britain and the holding of Irish people in jails throughout the country has been a feature of the British Government's attempts to subdue the Irish rebels from earliest times to the present. Some escapes and rescue attempts in England have gone drastically wrong, but notwithstanding that, several sensational escapes have been noted in history for their resourcefulness and their innovation. The Fenians believed that actions in Britain would be ultimately more beneficial to 'the cause' than any actions they might take in Ireland and so to promote this aim it was decided to detonate several bombs in England. The authorities clamped down straight away in an attempt to prevent the campaign from gaining further momentum. On 11 September 1867, Colonel Thomas J Kelly, Head of the IRB and Captain Timothy Deasy were arrested in Manchester. The Fenian movement had already been organised in Manchester and they soon hatched an elaborate plan to rescue their members from the clutches of their captors. On 19 September the prisoners were taken to the Courthouse. As they passed under a railway bridge in Manchester the Fenians held up the carriage. In their attempts to open the door the rescuers fired a shot into the lock. Unfortunately, Sergeant Brett, who was guarding the prisoners inside the carriage happened to be looking through the keyhole at the time. He fell mortally wounded. His keys were handed out, the doors opened and the two Fenians departed as quickly as they could. Mass arrests were made in the Irish quarters in Manchester and all known Fenian sympathisers were rounded up. On 28 October 1867, twenty-six people appeared before a special court in the city charged with helping in the rescue. On 23 November 1867 at Salford Jail three men were eventually hanged. William Phillip Allen, Michael Larkin and Michael O'Brien became immortalised in Irish history as the Manchester Martyrs with the song 'God Save Ireland.'

Within weeks, and following further arrests, another escape was planned. This time it was to be from Clerkenwell in London. Clerkenwell was a working class area in that city and had a large Irish population living in and around the jail. Feelings were running high at the time as a result of the triple execution and the Fenians decided to rescue two other major figures in the organisation, Ricard O'Sullivan Burke and Joseph Casey. The plan of action was to blow a hole in the perimeter wall while the prisoners were exercising in the adjacent yard. The Fenians could then be spirited away to safe houses. Unknown to those on the outside however the jail authorities had received prior knowledge about the escape attempt and subsequently changed the time of the exercise period. The day of the escape was Friday the thirteenth — a bad omen to many people. On that day (13 December 1867) the bomb was placed in position and the fuse was lit. When it exploded it blew not only a huge hole in the prison wall but the force of the explosion blew out in the other direction and demolished a row of workers houses. Twelve people died and one hundred and twenty were injured. On 20 April 1868, five men and one woman appeared before a London court charged with complicity in the rescue attempt. On 26 May 1868 one of those charged, Michael Barrett, was hanged outside Newgate Prison. His was the last public execution in England and thousands turned out to witness the hanging.

It was in a background such as this then that the internees from the 1918 period arrived in British prisons. Any further escapes would have to be planned meticulously, with an eye to preventing loss of life. On 17 May 1918, the British Government arrested scores of people in Ireland. Of those arrested seventy-three were transferred to jails in England and Wales. The most notable detainee among those transferred was Eamon De Valera. A proclamation by the British Government, justifying their actions, stated:

> *It has come to our knowledge that certain subjects of his Majesty*
> *the King, domiciled in Ireland, have conspired to enter into,*
> *treasonable communication with the German enemy...*

It was believed by the vast majority of people that the detentions were motivated more by the Republican movement's active opposition to conscription, at that time, than with any supposed plot with the Germans (The Conscription Bill had just been passed by the British House of Commons). Republicans had their own way of riding the storm — escape. The Republican prisoners after arriving in Britain were dispersed throughout several jails. The practice of bringing Irish prisoners over to Britain was a familiar tactic. As in 1916, use was made of the Frongach internment camp for those who took part in the rebellion in Dublin. On 22 January 1919, four detainees escaped from Usk Jail in Wales. Several weeks later on 3 February, Eamon De Valera and two others escaped from Lincoln Jail. Finally, six men escaped from Manchester. It did not end there, however, many other escapes did not come to fruition and many tunnels, quite literally, did not see the light of day but the planning continued.

Usk Jail was in the town of Usk near Monmoth in South Wales. The jail, prior to the escape, had witnessed a prolonged prison protest against criminalisation. Before long the authorities capitulated and soon the prisoners and their guards settled down in the harmonious surroundings of this Welsh town.

The escape plan began when one of the men managed to secure one of the cell door keys. Then with the help of smuggled nail files and ingenious manoeuvring, they were able to fashion another main key from the iron of a poker. The men thought that the best way to escape would be to scale the wall after letting themselves out of their cells with the keys. The construction of a handball-alley right next to the perimeter wall meant that they knew the exact height to make the rope-ladder and they also knew the exact shape of the coping on top of the wall. Everything ready, they now only had to wait on the most opportune moment. Then tragedy struck in the form of the flu epidemic. Many of the prisoners became seriously ill and after one of them, Dick Coleman, died from his illness, the authorities decided to move the prisoners to a more humane environment at Gloucester. When this happened the planners decided that the escape plan would have to be swung into effect immediately. Only four of the men, George Geraghty, Joseph McGrath, Herbert Mellows and Frank Shouldice, were fit to 'go out.' The initial plans for the mass escape had to be abandoned. Fifteen men remained behind, too weak to attempt to escape.

The Governor told the men that they would be moved the following morning and the OC negotiated an agreement with him that all the cell doors be left open that night so that the necessary preparations for the transfer could be completed. The escapees could not believe their luck when the Governor agreed to this request. Shortly after lock-up the four men emerged from their hiding place in the yard. The rest of the operation went so easily that the men thought that something was surely amiss. They sneaked over to the base of the wall where with the first swing of the rope they hooked the ladder to the top. The first one up the rope was Geraghty, quickly followed by Barney Mellows, Frank Shouldice and McGrath. The last to go over was Geraghty. It was later revealed that the four men were almost immediately captured for they had only reached the road to Pontypool when they bumped into four warders going on duty. One of the warders, a man called Lovell, was a regular guard at the jail but he did not recognise the men and they hastened along the road until they reached the Pontypool railway junction where they hoped to catch the Fishguard Express. Since they had not coordinated their escape with the IRA on the outside, it seemed that this was where their plan was going to fall into disarray. They found that the train did not stop at Pontypool and assuming that it would stop on down the line at Pilemile they continued their journey, always aware that their escape might have already been discovered. Upon arriving at Pilemile, they discovered the station locked for the night. The town was deserted. The four men headed for a local hotel, where, posing as Americans, the receptionist directed them to a car owner called Evans who would drive them to Newport. Back at Usk Jail their escape had not yet been discovered. Everyone had been finishing packing while the warders settled down to what they believed was an easy night on duty.

The train to Liverpool was sitting at the platform at Newport Station when the escapees arrived next morning. They thanked their taxi driver and he went off. Then, quite by chance, they had another stroke of luck. There on the platform they noticed a prominent Republican from Ireland who happened to be on an intelligence gathering mission. The men told him of their escape and the man at once gave them some cash to help them on their way to Liverpool where they remained in a safe house before being smuggled back to Ireland by boat. On 22 January the British papers carried descriptions of the men;

> *WANTED*
>
> *Sinn Féin prison breakers. George Geraghty (40), dark complexion, heavy dark moustache, weight 11 stone, 6ft. in height; Joseph McGrath (28), clean shaven, pale complexion, loose lipped and drawls, 6ft. in height, 12 stone; Herbert Mellows (28), clean shaven, hair long and light brown, pale complexion, wears glasses, his overcoat is rather too long for him, 10 stone; Frank Shouldice (25), round boyish face, fresh complexion, appears shy, has little Irish accent, 6ft. in height, 12 stone. The others have much accent.*

A short time after this successful escape another equally successful escape by Republican prisoners embarrassed the Government yet again. Yet again, Irishmen showed that they still had the ingenuity and courage to defy and outwit their captors. The Republican prisoners in Lincoln Jail were allowed to associate freely with each other at exercise times and it was while walking around the yard at Lincoln that they hatched their plans to escape. Their initial plans seemed to be too ambitious. They involved an intricate amount of planning both inside and outside the jail. Firstly one of the doors in the exercise yard seemed to lead directly onto the surrounding green fields. It was in effect a perimeter wall. If they could get keys to get out of their cells, then keys for the jail corridors and gates and finally a key for this door in the wall, then they would be free. One of the main factors which helped their plans come to fruition was the fact that the IRA needed to free De Valera to represent the voice of Ireland at the forthcoming Peace Conference. Not only that but the IRA had developed tremendously in both Ireland and Britain.

The entire resources of the IRA Headquarters in Dublin and the IRA in Britain were involved in the escape under the able direction of Michael Collins. Ultimately, three cakes containing three keys, blanks, files and key-cutting equipment were smuggled into the jail. A rope ladder and relays of motor cars were all put into operation for this important rescue. Initially, the chaplain of Lincoln unwittingly encouraged the first stages of the plan. He left a key carelessly sitting on a table in the sacristy of the chapel. De Valera served Mass along with him and on noticing the key quickly took an impression by pressing it into a lump of warm candle wax. Sean Milroy sent out a sketch of the key on a Christmas card. The prisoners believed this was the master key. The key was replicated and sent back hidden inside a cake, the most traditional way of smuggling used by Republicans. However, it was soon found that this was not the key they needed. A lot of toing and froing followed with copies of keys being made and tested accordingly. Finally it was the work of Paddy de Loughrey which saved the day. He dismantled one of the jail locks and soon got to work making the master key which would ultimately lead to freedom.

In the meantime, the IRA, under the supervision of Collins had been gathering information about the movements of troops and civilians in the vicinity of the jail. The exercise-yard door opened directly onto the front gates of a military hospital and subsequently there was always a lot of activity both day and night. Collins did not believe that this would be a hindrance, in fact it would help their plans. The surrounding fields were used by courting couples and as such no attention was paid to people loitering in that immediate area.

On the night prearranged for the escape, Michael Collins, Harry Boland and Frank Kelly arrived at the jail which stood several hundred yards on the outskirts of the town. All three were armed. A relay of cars were in place to take the escapees to Worksop, from Worksop to Sheffield and from Sheffield to Manchester, where they would take shelter in safe houses. Boland gave three quick flashes from a torch in the direction of the upper storey of Lincoln prison . As they awaited in the darkness, they soon noticed the return signal. The escape was about to begin. Three Republican prisoners, Eamon De Valera, Sean Milroy and Sean McGarry made their way through the jail, carefully locking all the doors and gates behind them as they passed. Collins and Boland approached the side gate. When they reached it they heard the three men on the other side. As Collins tried to open the last gate he was horrified to find that the key stuck. He forced it and the key broke. De Valera thrust de Loughrey's master key into the lock and the broken head fell out the other side. The gate opened with a loud creak and the three men stepped out into the field to the warm embrace of Collins and Boland. All five headed off towards where the cars were waiting, greeting the courting couples as they went.

The most difficult part of the escape bid still awaited them. All five squeezed into the waiting taxi and were driven to Lincoln town centre where Collins and Boland got off to catch a train to London. The taxi brought the men to Worksop where another taxi was waiting to take them to Sheffield and from there by private car to Manchester and shelter. Their escape was not discovered until two hours later. Even though a huge security operation was quickly swung into operation, the prisoners disappeared into the mists. Before long they were back in Ireland breathing the sweet air of freedom.

Then, in October, six prisoners escaped from Strangeways Jail in Manchester. The third sensational escape by 'German Plot' prisoners took place on 25 October 1919, in broad daylight, from under the noses of the prison authorities in Manchester. The last Irish political prisoners to escape from Manchester were the two Fenians in 1867. They were never recaptured.

Those who escaped were: Piarais Béaslaí, Austin Stack, D P Walsh, Paddy McCarthy, Con Connolly and Sean Doran. The main instigator of the escape was Piarais Béaslaí. At the time Strangeways held all the Irish prisoners who had been imprisoned at Belfast's Crumlin Road Prison. While in Belfast they had engaged in a rigid protest with the authorities for recognition of the fact that they should be classified as political prisoners. Austin Stack was the representative of the Republicans at the jail and Sean Doran was the man around whom the Belfast Jail riots centred in 1918 .

At length, they were eventually transferred to Strangeways where all their previous demands were met by the British prison authorities. There were eleven Republican prisoners in Strangeways before Piarais Béaslaí arrived. Immediately upon arrival he put his escape plans into operation and at once decided that a replication of the recent daytime escape at Mountjoy would have the best chance of success. Strangeways Prison was in Manchester, and the getaway from such a strange place could not be planned as easily as Belfast or Dublin. Furthermore, the Irish prisoners were closely guarded here. The yard in which they took their exercise was in the centre of the prison and surrounded by jail buildings. At their evening exercise period, the routine was quite different. On that occasion they exercised in a yard that was enclosed by a ring of high railings. Outside these railings there was a forty foot high wall, from which extended rows of spikes facing downwards, to deter any attempt at escaping over the wall. A major blunder had been spotted by the ever inquisitive Republicans. Further down the wall, facing the wing of the women's hospital, a section was without these hazardous spikes. To get to that section their access was barred by just a six foot high railing.

Michael Collins was soon contacted and he was asked to help the prisoners find what was on the other side of the wall without the spikes. The outline of their intended escape was also communicated to Collins. Collins in turn sent Rory O'Connor to examine the outside of the jail. Communiques and maps were smuggled in to the prisoners, hidden in cakes and foodstuffs, until finally they had built up a picture of the operation that lay before them. To their delight they discovered that the wall without the spikes led directly onto a small side street, off a main thoroughfare.

October 25th, was the date finally chosen for the breakout. The prisoners were let out for their evening exercise period at 5.00pm. One warder was assigned to watch the six prisoners. Once they were let out of their cells after supper, they immediately over-powered the guard. Tied and gagged, he was locked into a cell. The six men immediately jumped over the railing and made their way to the gap in the spikes. Once there they threw over a stone. This signal was almost immediately returned when someone threw back a rope. To the men's frustration the rope did not come down far enough and dangled high out of reach. The six men thought they were sure to be caught as they were standing in the open yard in full view of anyone who should happen to look out from the hospital wing. The second throw of the rope was still unsuccessful. Once again it caught on something and remained high out of reach. Thinking that they would have to abandon their escape, the men were relieved when they heard ladders being put up the other side of the wall. They saw the face of one of their rescuers looking over. Freeing the rope he immediately dropped it down to the prisoners and before long the six men were scrambling up and over the wall to freedom.

More than twenty men had been posted outside the jail, where they successfully held up everyone who attempted to pass by. Nobody offered the party of men any resistance as the escapees fled the scene, making their getaway in hired taxis and on bicycles. Several prisoners managed to get lost amidst the confusion but they eventually got to safe houses in the immediate area where the Manchester Irish gave them a hearty welcome. Before long the escapees were back in Ireland.

One year later Sean Doran was recaptured and deported to Strangeways. McCarthy was shot dead by the Black and Tans. D P Walsh was captured in Scotland and he too was sent back to Strangeways. All the others evaded capture. As the conflict in Ireland had not been satisfactorily concluded, it was inevitable that the British prisons would once again begin to receive political prisoners. When it is explained that the new design for prisons was to create a prison within a prison, it can then be appreciated how difficult it was to plan and execute an escape in Britain. Not only are the secure units, which have finally evolved from the old Victorian style prison, jails within jails, but the prison complex itself is situated in an area which would be regarded as extremely hostile to Irish political prisoners — Republican or otherwise. The difficulties in escaping from Britain therefore increased dramatically.

Coupled with these difficulties was the fact that the population of Irish political prisoners in British jails was quite small compared to that in the North of Ireland. This led to a feeling of isolation which the British prison authorities further sought to instil in these prisoners. The British Government have been aware of these tactics since their first involvement in Ireland. They had used Fort George in Scotland to incarcerate the United Irishmen, then as the option of sending prisoners to penal settlements in Australia was curtailed, they eventually developed a strategy closer to home. After their involvement in the Boer War and the development of internment camps, the prison strategists had a wealth of experience to draw upon. By 1919 people arrested for 'treasonable' offences in Ireland were being shipped off to jails and camps in Britain on a regular basis. The strategy of 'ghosting' prisoners was also established at this stage. 'Ghosting' prisoners entailed shifting them around from prison to prison before they could settle down in any one place. It was a deliberate attempt to increase the feeling of isolation in a prisoner. It was soon realised that in order to have complete control it would be necessary to establish special wings within the jails to house what were termed high risk prisoners. These prisoners could then be isolated from the majority of other prisoners in the jails. Irish political prisoners were regarded as high security risk and were therefore held in these 'maximum security' conditions. Although these conditions developed gradually, they can be seen clearly against the background of potential escapes by the prisoners who continued to try to outwit their jailers.

In 1956 an elaborate attempt to free Cathal Goulding from Wakefield prison was aborted at the last minute after the prison authorities appeared to have got wind of the escape attempt. This was followed three years later on 19 February 1959, with the successful escape of 24 year-old James Murphy from Wakefield Prison. Murphy, a native of Castledermot, Co Kildare, had been given a life sentence along with two other Irishmen, John Doyle and Donal Murphy at the Berkshire Assizes, in Reading in 1955. They had been convicted of taking part in a raid on a British Army depot at Arborfield, Berkshire, and taking sixty-six guns and eighty-five thousand rounds of ammunition. Murphy had scaled the twenty foot high perimeter wall during the night. On the other side a car was waiting. He quickly changed into civilian clothing and was driven off to Liverpool, from where he was smuggled back to Ireland within days. The prison authorities were reeling with embarrassment at this latest escape and quickly brought into motion a plan which they had been working on for several years. That plan was to introduce a category system within the prisons whereby maximum security prisoners would be held at specially designed maximum security prisons. The categorisation system was introduced in the wake of a series of other embarrassing escapes in the 1960's which culminated in the escape of the spy George Blake.

Back in Ireland the 'troubles' as they became known, continued. By the late 1960s Nationalists in the North of Ireland began agitating for civil rights. The situation which developed led to one of the most violent periods in Ireland's history. British soldiers were soon patrolling the streets of Belfast and Derry and troop levels continued to rise. Buildings were requisitioned and turned into fortresses and the relatively quiet skies over the Six Counties became alive with the constant whirr of helicopters and spotter planes. In the early 1970s, the IRA instigated a series of bomb attacks in Britain. In the wake of these attacks there were many arrests and court appearances with the result that the Republican population in prisons began to rise dramatically. Several escapes were attempted but failed. One such attempt, which involved Gerry Kelly, from Belfast, took place at Wormwood Scrubs. He had been convicted for planting bombs in London in March 1973. When sentenced he refused to wear prison uniform and was in turn refused all privileges. He eventually took part in a hunger strike with several others, demanding to be repatriated to Ireland. This strike almost led to the deaths of the striking prisoners until the government began to force feed them. Kelly was moved back, along with the Price sisters, Dolores and Marion, and Hugh Feeny in 1976.

The history of escapes in Britain has been an unfolding story of intrigue and espionage, as the government tried to infiltrate the IRA and thereby thwart any operations they had planned. On 6 March 1974, Kenneth Lennon and Patrick O'Brien were charged with conspiracy to help three Irishmen, The Luton Three, escape from Winson Green Prison after Lennon was arrested in the prison car park. Plans of the jail were allegedly found at his home. On 13 April 1974, Kenneth Lennon's body was found in a ditch in Surrey. He had been shot in the head. Three days previous to his death he made a seventeen page statement to a representative of the National Council for Civil Liberties in which he claimed he was a Special Branch informer. He claimed that he was being paid £20.00 per month and he believed that he was going to be killed, either by the IRA or by the Special Branch themselves. Back in Ireland, the prison system was constantly faced with the reality of escaping political prisoners, and the government knew their propaganda value. Such incidents undermined their ability to control the growing prison population in Ireland and now the prisons in Britain were faced with the same scenario.

The British Government believed they could control the prison situation more easily by their categorisation system coupled with their policy of ghosting the Irish political prisoners around a network of eight prisons. They included Albany, Parkhurst, Wormwood Scrubs, Longlartin, Gartree, Hull, Wakefield and Durham. These establishments which were then used to house Republican, or 'maximum security risk' prisoners were thought to have been virtually escape-proof. Since 1977, not a single prisoner had escaped from any of these special wings. It became increasingly hard to plan any type of rescue as the government implemented their isolation policy. Prisoners were frequently 'ghosted' away during the night to another prison without their prior knowledge. This constant moving of the prisoners meant that it became extremely difficult to gain an intimate knowledge of the prison.

There had been several attempts to escape but each attempt had become increasingly difficult to coordinate. In 1978, there was an attempt to escape from Parkhurst on the Isle of Wight. It failed, but it was only a matter of time before the prisoners would succeed. That success came at Brixton in December 1980 and caused major embarrassment for the British Government. It involved one of their most prized prisoners, Gerard Tuite, a native of Mountnugent in Co Cavan. It was a double embarrassment because it took place at the height of the Armagh/Long Kesh hunger strike in December 1980. Brixton, at the time of Tuite's escape was Europe's biggest remand centre. Twenty-five year old, Tuite and seven others, had appeared in court on various charges ranging from bombings at a Greenwich gasworks and an oil depot at Ganvey Island in Essex, to car bombings in London and plotting the escape of Brian Keenan from Brixton prison. Brian Keenan a native of Belfast was alleged to have been one of the main IRA personnel involved in some of the bombings carried out by those who were captured after the Balcombe Street siege. He had been sentenced to eighteen years.

The other two escapers were non political prisoners who were being held for armed robberies. They were Stanley Thompson and James Moody. Thompson surrendered four days after his escape, while Moody remained at large and was shot dead in a London street in 1993.

According to police reports it was believed that Moody broke through the wall into Thompson's cell and then the two made a hole into Tuite's cell. A third hole was then made through a fifteen inch thick outside wall at Tuite's cell at 'D' Wing, where all three men got through, some time between 2.00am and 5.00am. This led them out onto a flat roof at the prison. Building work had been in progress at the prison and the men were able to take some scaffolding planks from nearby 'C' Wing to help them get over the perimeter wall into the street. All three were wearing their own civilian clothes and not prison uniforms which meant that they were able to disappear into the London street without raising much alarm. Their absence was not discovered until the warders unlocked the cells next morning. Hundreds of colour posters with two pictures of Tuite were distributed throughout London stating, "This man must be caught." The government claimed that Tuite was a master of disguise and as such his wanted posters contained two photographs, one showing him with long hair and clean shaven while the other showed him with short hair and a beard. Tuite was said to have used several aliases.

Tuite's trial was due to begin at the Old Bailey on 5 March 1981. Despite a massive search he successfully returned to Ireland. He was subsequently arrested and charged in the Dublin Special Court in March 1982 under the Criminal Law Jurisdiction Act 1976 and was sentenced to ten years imprisonment the following July. He was the first person convicted at the Dublin court for an alleged offence outside the jurisdiction of Ireland. At the Old Bailey trial on 5 March 1981, two women admitted conspiring to effect the escape of Brian Keenan. The prosecution alleged that Keenan was to be rescued by armed men in a hijacked helicopter while he exercised in a wire enclosure at the prison known as 'the Cage'. Mrs Margaret Parrat had made hiring inquiries, while Miss Jacqueline O'Malley had already booked one of the helicopters for a dry run. Both women were arrested after the helicopters were hired. Those who also faced conspiracy charges were Bobby Storey, Bobby Campbell and Richard Glenholmes, all from Belfast.

It had now become clear that the planners had been targeting for potential breeches in prison security and it would only be a matter of time before they would succeed in effecting another spectacular escape. The government, already severely stretched with its prison policy in Northern Ireland, began to look more closely at its prison security. They realised that there was by this stage, a well-established network of friends and supporters on whom the prisoners could rely. On top of that the originally hostile environment of Britain was changing into a multi-racial society with less prejudicial views on Ireland and Irish people. As 'the troubles' continued in Northern Ireland, IRA attacks also continued in Britain against what they perceived to be legitimate targets. On 2 October 1990 two men, Pearse McAuley from Strabane and Nessan Quinlivan from Limerick, were arrested at a public car park near Stonehenge in Wiltshire. Both men were taken to Paddington Green police station in London and after six days in police custody they appeared before a court charged with conspiring to cause explosions. Over the following weeks the police carried out raids on Irish clubs and apartments belonging to Irish people. McAuley and Quinlivan, meanwhile, were remanded in custody to Brixton prison, pending a date for their trial. They were never to make that appearance. On Sunday, 7 July 1991, as they were being escorted from the chapel at the jail, the two men managed to escape.

The escape caused a furore in the Commons as Labour's deputy leader, Roy Hattersley, called for a full enquiry. It was also revealed that senior managers of the prison service had been warned of the possibility of an escape after guns and explosives were smuggled in to Belfast prison in late 1989. What made matters worse was the fact that the report brought particular attention to how they believed the weapons were smuggled in to the prison — in the hollowed out sole of a baseball boot (similar to that which McAuley was said to have been wearing that day).

On the morning of the escape, both men were being escorted back to the secure unit. Being a Sunday, a more relaxed regime existed at the prison with less than half the normal amount of prison warders on duty. McAuley allegedly bent down to tie his lace and as he stood up again he produced a pistol from his shoe. A number of shots were fired to keep the warders at bay. Taking the keys of the escorting warders they opened the gates out to the prison's main courtyard. The two men then scaled the outer wall of the prison and made off towards the front of the prison at Jebb Avenue. Here they took a prison warder's car. Their passage was blocked by another car after the driver realised what was happening. This car was abandoned at the top of Brixton Hill where they hijacked a Vauxhall Cavalier and drove to the rear of Lambeth Town hall. Eyewitnesses said they then saw both men take a black cab to Baker Street underground station.

All sea and air ports were immediately put on red alert as descriptions of the men were wired to the police. The two men were back in Ireland several days later where they eluded the Gardaí until their arrests in Tipperary and Dublin in April 1993. After a court appearance, both were remanded in custody to Portlaoise jail.

Escape plans in Britain continued unabated. In 1993 two men who eventually escaped from another prison, were involved in an unsuccessful escape attempt from Parkhurst jail on the Isle of Wight. They were both transferred to Whitemoor prison in Cambridgeshire. In a scene reminiscent of that which occurred at Derry prison after the 1921 Truce was signed, five Republican prisoners and another man, tried to shoot their way out of the jail only ten days after the IRA called a ceasefire in September 1994. The six men were Paul Magee, Liam McCotter, Gilbert McNamee, Peter Sherry and Liam O'Dwyer and a non political prisoner Andrew Russell. All were recaptured within hours of their escape which took place under cover of darkness at 8.00pm on Friday, 9 September 1994. According to newspaper reports at the time, the prisoners had cut through the fence that seals off the secure unit from the perimeter wall. One warder gave chase and was shot and wounded. After scaling three thirty-five foot walls using knotted sheets, four were immediately recaptured when they were threatened by dog handlers. Two of the Republican prisoners, Liam O'Dwyer and Peter Sherry, had breached the security fence and went to ground about a mile from the prison. They had lost the element of surprise, however, and realised it would only be a matter of time before they would be recaptured. They were eventually discovered by police using sniffer dogs and helicopters in a massive search of the area. Their attempt to escape came at a delicate juncture in the 'Peace Process' but any claims that suggested that it was the end of the ceasefire were dismissed by both the Republican Movement and the

British Government. who described the incident as a "hiccup". Britain's Home Secretary, Michael Howard ordered an inquiry to ascertain how the two guns used in the escape bid had been smuggled into the jail, and, whether or not the prisoners had help from warders working at the prison.

> *The Gaols of France are snug and warm,*
> *And British cells are airy,*
> *But Irishmen think the reverse*
> *Which proves it quite contrary.*
>
> *In Strangeways Gaol did England fail,*
> *With locks and chains to bind them,*
> *And o'er the top did quickly drop*
> *And left the gaol behind them.*

(An old Dublin ballad celebrating the escape from Strangeways Prison.)

The morning after the internment camp at Long Kesh was burned.

15. Lucky Escape.

Some people who achieved their freedom did so by pure luck. They are the people who saw their opportunity and pounced on it without any premeditated planning. One of the most famous Irishmen to have escaped on such an unplanned opportunity was Sean McBride, later to become Irish Foreign Minister and 1974 Nobel Peace prize winner. He made a run for it when the lorry conveying him to Kilmainham lost its way in Dublin in 1923.

General Tom Barry also escaped when the same lucky opportunities came his way. He had tried to escape from Mountjoy dressed in a Free State Army coat in March 1922. Reclassified as a potential escapee, he was transferred from Mountjoy to Gormanstown camp. On arrival, he walked straight across to the other side of the camp, where he crawled under the barbed wire entanglements when no one was looking. History is replete with such incidents. Prisoners escaped in transit and even got away from military bases, once their captors dropped their guard. One of the first recorded incident in a similar category took place at Belfast almost two hundred years ago. 1798 is a year in Irish history when the ideals of republicanism were extolled as the political and moral answers to Ireland's troubles. Fraternity and unity were being encouraged in France at the time and Ireland soon followed suit. The rebellion was viciously put down by the British Yeomanry and the brutality of the period has long been remembered in songs such as *Henry Joy* and *Boolavogue*.

It was during this period that we learn of the escape of one of the United men from the clutches of his tormentors in Belfast city centre. His escape, concealment and subsequent leaving of Ireland, for exile in another land, was a feature which has been repeated in Irish history right down to the present day. Most fled to America in the belief that they would be safe there. Others chose the European continent and yet more decided to stay and try to carry on undetected in their own land, refusing to be coerced to a new life abroad.

On 2 July 1798, William Keane, a prisoner charged with treason and rebellion, made his escape from confinement. A general search was made immediately throughout all the houses in the town of Belfast, and a notice from James Derham, Colonel Commandant was published calling on the inhabitants of Belfast,

> *to assist in discovering and delivering up the said Keane, who is now concealed or harboured in some part of this town. And shall it be found hereafter, that said traitor has been concealed by any person or persons, or by the knowledge or connivance of any person or persons of this town and its neighbourhood, or that they or any of them have known of the place of concealment, and shall not have given notice thereof to the commandant of this town, such person's house will be burned and the owner thereof hanged!*

Antrim had risen in response to the call of the United Irishmen but in the end their hopes and ideals were defeated. Most of those involved were either captured or killed on the spot. Many more were conveyed to Belfast where they were court-martialled and sentenced. So many were brought into the town that an improvised guardhouse was opened in a building at the corner of Cooney's Court, off Ann Street and every evening the prisoners caught that day were confined therein. At the same time a curfew order was enforced on the inhabitants of Belfast. They were confined to their homes after 9.00pm each night and the town and all its inhabitants remained under martial law. The prison ship, *Postlethwaite*, was moored in Belfast Lough to hold the insurgent United Irishmen. Several people were taken out after their court-martial and hanged at the Market House. The first was James Dickey. He was tried at the Exchange Rooms and executed on 26 June 1798, outside the Market House, his head was cut off and raised on a spike above the said building. John Storey was hanged on 29 June, Hugh Grimes on 6 July, Henry Joy McCracken on 7 July and Henry Byres on 11 July. The executions continued for quite some time. *The Town Book of Belfast* by R M Young, records an execution in 1799;

> *17 May - George Dixon (who called himself General Holt) having been found guilty by the court-martial of treason and rebellion, robbing his Majesty's soldiers of their arms, and assisting the rebels at Randalstown on the 7 June 1798, etc. was this day brought from the prison to the Market House and after spending some time in devotion, was launched into eternity a little after one o'clock ... like some similar culprits who had lately suffered, he would not let his face be covered.*

William Keane, had made good his escape after being sentenced to die in a similar fashion. He was never recaptured. His story did not end there and it was recalled many years later to an American pressman by the daughter of Samuel Neilson, herself an elderly lady at the time of writing. She recalled;

"When the military rabble broke into *The Northern Star* office and threw the type out onto the streets and arrested the printers, there was one among them named William Keane. Of course they were all United Irishmen, but they had proof against Keane, and I think he was tried and sentenced to death. The day before the execution he begged to be allowed to see a priest as he was a Catholic. There was a priest in the prison for treason, but he was very sick, so sick that he could not get out of bed. Willie Keane would have to go to him. But before allowing him into the priest's room they made him take off his shoes and coat, so that if he escaped he would attract attention and be arrested. 'I am suffocating. Open the window, Willie, and give me a breath of air,' said the priest as soon as Willie Keane entered the room. It was not a regular prison - all the regular prisons were full - but a house the Government had turned into a prison, so there were no bars on the windows. His confession ended, Willie Keane climbed through the window and made off for his life. As he had to pass a barrack, he knew that he would attract attention and be arrested. He saw a man in a backyard and said to him, 'Would you give a boy your shoes and coat to save his life?'

'Faith and I would' replied the man, looking at him and suspecting what was the matter. Willie Keane put on the man's coat and shoes, and went down past the barracks whistling *Croppies Lie Down*. He went down to the bridge and stood under it up to is neck in water until the next morning, when his friends got him smuggled away on board a vessel, and finally he got to America, where he became a wealthy and respectable citizen."

Chances like this have constantly presented themselves through the years. They are basically oversights by those entrusted with prison security. One period of Ireland's history which led to several of these types of escapes was during the 1922 Civil War. As the prisons began to fill and their populations began to grow very quickly, this expansion was matched by the subsequent rise in escapes and escape attempts. Plans for most escapes took a long time to convert into reality. The story of the attempted escapes from Mountjoy prison at this time are representative of the frustration of the escapees. Frustrations at constantly being caught.

In August 1922, an attempt was made to tunnel into Mountjoy Prison from 28 Innisfallen Parade, a neighbouring street. The occupants of the house left the tunnellers to their own devices while they went off on holiday. The tunnel was discovered on 10 August. After this plan failed, the prisoners decided on another plan. On 10 October 1922, an escape was attempted which involved overpowering the guards. A gun had been smuggled in and a couple of dummy guns had been carved. The plan was to hold up the military police inside 'C' Wing of the jail and get the keys. The prisoners would then gain entrance to the guard room, hold the soldiers who were on duty there, and disarm them. Then with the hostages secure, the keys and guns in hand, they would let themselves out through the gates. The plan was fraught with difficulties but went ahead nevertheless. It was clear, that once the first stage of the plan was put into operation, things were not going to turn out as planned. Simon Donnelly was the man who was to set the plan in motion. It was his job to confront the first soldier on guard duty and disarm him. However, the soldier, once challenged by Donnelly, went for his gun. Donnelly shot him. In the subsequent commotion the soldiers emerged from the guard room and fired on the prisoners from the behind the safety of a locked gate. Commandant Peadar Breslin, one of the prisoners, died after being hit by a stray bullet. Two policemen, Constable James Gallagher and Constable James Kearns along with the soldier Private Thomas Gaffney also died. It was after this botched attempt to escape that it was decided to have someone tunnel in to the prison. This plot was also discovered fairly quickly but another attempt was soon made to tunnel in, this time from Glengariff Parade in November . Two other tunnels had been attempted out of 'A' and 'C' Wings of the jail but, unfortunately, they were discovered. The novel idea of tunnelling in was later used at Belfast but it too was discovered. On 8 December 1922, Rory O'Connor, Liam Mellows, Dick Barrett and Joe McKelvey were executed by the Free State Authorities. Mountjoy became the scene of sorrow and horror for many who were involved in the establishment of an Irish Republic.

Sean McBride was one man who was there when the executions were carried out. His own father had been taken from his cell in Kilmainham and shot in a similar fashion after the 1916 Rising. Sean McBride had been in many of Ireland's jails and his knowledge and experience were tremendous incentives to other prisoners who met him. Some months after the executions he was transferred to Newbridge where he was noted for an audacious escape attempt. He tried to escape in the swill cart which left the prison kitchen on a daily basis. He was caught by the sentry at the gate who probed around the contents of the cart before letting it pass. After his escape attempt was discovered he was sent back to Mountjoy. McBride did not give up trying to break out. Flaws in security were looked at in great detail and every opportunity for escape was carefully examined. Their observations resulted in a selection of the prisoners digging a tunnel. The entrance to the tunnel was high up in the building near the top of the tall stone chimney stack. Some of those involved in this escape were Dr Tom Powell, Tony Woods, Peadar O'Donnell and Tom Maguire. Once inside the chimney the men used a ladder made from sheets reinforced with wire to let themselves down to the basement, where the prisoners began the tunnel proper. All the digging was carried out between roll calls and all the surplus earth was hauled up from the dig and scattered around the roof space. The tunnelling was near to completion when some of the other prisoners embarked on a hunger strike. Those who were taking part in this hunger strike were not aware of the planned escape. However, as the hunger strike developed, and winter was beginning to set in, the prison authorities decided to turn on the heating. When nothing would work they went up into the roof-space to investigate what they thought would be a mere plumbing problem. To their delight and the prisoner's dismay the attempted breakout was discovered. After an internal inquiry those believed to have been involved in the tunnel were transferred to Kilmainham by lorry. Among those to be moved was Sean McBride. The lorry carrying McBride lost its escort as it turned into Berkley Road in Dublin. As the captain stopped to discuss what to do McBride made a run for it, quickly followed by a fellow prisoner, and OC of the jail, Mick Price. They were never recaptured.

It is only when you look at the amount of times the prisoners at Mountjoy had tried to escape that such lucky breaks can be appreciated. At the same time as McBride's escape, luck shone on a young Dublin youth called George Gilmore who was also being held at Mountjoy. Luck and a momentary lapse in security was all that was required. His dash for freedom was recorded in Ernie O'Malley's book, *The Singing Flame*. In this book he tells how workmen had left a ladder against a perimeter wall. Gilmore made a dash for the ladder and taking his chance scaled the wall while a soldier shot at him. He luckily made it unscathed.

The courts have frequently provided unexpected chances for escapers. Courts and jails are, of course, inextricably linked in the processing of prisoners and their journey to and from such establishments have often proved to be the most vulnerable link in the chain of security. Frank Carty used this weakness to his advantage in Glasgow as did the Fenians in Manchester. The threat and possibility of a rescue, or an escape attempt, has resulted in many of today's courts using precautions of even greater magnitude than the prisons themselves. One of the most sensational and successful breakouts from a courthouse took place in 1922 during the Civil War. On that occasion, twenty-three men successfully evaded recapture after they managed to overpower the guards and, seizing their rifles and ammunition they made their escape from Kanturk Courthouse in County Cork. Some of the most daring court escapes took place in more recent times. As the troubles in the North gained momentum, the subsequent increase in the prison population led to an increase in the frequency of escape attempts, some of which were highly successful.

In 1975, one such sensational escape hit the headlines when twelve Republican prisoners escaped from the Courthouse in Newry. Many of those who escaped on this occasion were being brought before the court charged with escaping on a previous occasion. The group were nicknamed 'The Trevor Hill twelve' and had been described by the RUC as high-security prisoners.

The story behind this particular escape reveals the flaws which ultimately occur within a system which had developed to such an extent that it had become cumbersome. One year before the escape, another batch of prisoners had been brought to Newry Courthouse for attempting to escape from the prison hospital at Long Kesh. After being led into the Courthouse, they were placed in a room along with three prison warders, before being called before the judge. Inside this room was a door which led to a small toilet. One of the prisoners entered this room and when he came out again, he told his mate to go in and 'check out' the window.

Outside this window was a series of rusty bars, beyond which was a small enclosed courtyard and then the perimeter fence. The bottom of the bars were almost rusted through. The prisoner pulled up the window, but try as he may, he could not break the bars. He came back in to the room again where the three warders were sitting and sat down. He knew in his heart that an escape from this window would be easily achieved with just a little planning. He could not act quickly enough because of the presence of the three warders in the room. Before long the men were brought into the court and were back in their Cage at Long Kesh again. Back in the hut they discussed what they had seen and sat down to hatch their breakout. They knew there was an RUC man who patrolled the courtyard and if they could overpower the warders in the room and the officer in the yard, then they had a chance.

On 11 March 1975, the public had other things on their minds. The IRA were into their second month of a ceasefire, and the newspapers were filled with reports and counter reports of the UDA's incendiary bombing of the Donegal fishing fleet at Greencastle harbour, and the INLA/OIRA feud. On that day also, an organised stoppage by the Farmers Action Group protesting against beef prices led to traffic disruption on all the roads in Northern Ireland. Their action meant that thousands of schoolchildren had an unexpected holiday but as it turned out that was not the only unexpected event to take place before the day was over.

The proceedings at Newry Courthouse were scheduled to go ahead as normal, regardless of the traffic disruption. The farmers had blocked the road at Ashgrove, and as a result, Judge James Brown, who was to have sat that morning, was airlifted by a British Army helicopter at Banbridge. The judge and the clerk of the court touched down at Downshire Road one hundred yards inside the barrier. Meanwhile, a convoy of prisoners set off from the Maze, about twenty miles away. After negotiating with the protesters at the barricades it was agreed to let the convoy, along with its police and military escort, pass through a side road which meant taking a five mile detour. Back in Newry, barristers abandoned their cars close to the protest barriers and walked the short distance to the Courthouse.

The batch of twelve men who had been brought to Newry Court that morning, had been charged with attempted escapes from the Compounds. They were in two batches, six for attempting to escape from the football pitch and six who tried to escape from the camp, dressed as British soldiers. Any of the previous plans for escaping from the court had been abandoned due to unforeseen problems on the outside. It was almost a year since the hospital escapees had visited Newry Court and had first noticed the breech in security. They thought that it would have been repaired by now. On their arrival the prisoners noticed that the usual routine had changed. Instead of the warders being locked in the same room as them, they now stayed outside in the hall, leaving the prisoners locked in the room by themselves. That was not the only mistake the warders made, for the door into the room did not have a peephole, which is common in jail-cell doors. The prisoners were literally left to their own devices. They had to think and act quickly because they knew that an RUC man would be on patrol in the court yard. They had no idea how much time they had or if there was now more than one RUC man on patrol. The prisoners quickly tore down the rusty bars round the window. Before long everyone was out in the yard, and after climbing up onto an electricity transformer they were able to make it up and over the security fence. The drop on the far side of the fence was around thirty feet and one of the escapers, Philip McMahon, broke his leg in the fall. They immediately rushed to the neighbouring garage forecourt where they commandeered a car. Everyone squeezed in. McMahon, who had by this stage realised that his leg was broken, had to persevere with the pain as most of the men jumped into the back of the car, on top of him. Driving away from the scene as quickly as possible, they made a wrong turn and ended up in a dead end street which had been blocked off with 'dragon's teeth'. They at once got out and commandeered another car which brought them over the border. Two cars were later found, one at the Warrenpoint Road and the other, at Flagstaff not far from the border. A message written with soap on the mirror in the Courthouse read .... "Up the IRA."

Once the alarm was raised, police and soldiers were called in from around the town to help in the search. Checkpoints were placed on all the main roads and Gardaí and Irish Army troops also put checkpoints on the other side of the border. Two of those who escaped were almost immediately recaptured, after they had been spotted by a British Army helicopter as they made their way along a back road which led to the border. The two men were John McMullan from the Lower Falls and Terence 'Cleaky' Clarke from Ardoyne. Clarke had previously escaped from Belfast Prison with the 'Crumlin Kangaroos' and he and McMullan had been facing charges that morning for attempting to escape from the football pitch at Long Kesh.

The others who escaped were: John Quigley and William McGuigan from the New Lodge, Philip McMahon and Hugh Clarke from Andersonstown, Martin Clement Ferris from Newry, Malachy McCarry from the Lower Falls, Eugene Fanning from the Bone, Paddy Braniff and Larry Marley from Ardoyne, and Gerard Fitzgerald from Ballymurphy.

During searches of premises the British Army raided the Cathedral in Newry. This was seen as an infringement of the ceasefire and desperate attempts to resolve the situation resulted in the IRA making a statement that the ceasefire was intact. The British Army apologised to the Canon of the Cathedral for any inconvenience.

The courts became a regular scene of attempted escapes. Most of them were spur of the moment decisions and so the majority of them were unsuccessful. In 1973, the Chief of Security at the Belfast Magistrate Court, was publicly stating that staffing levels were insufficient to handle the rise in prisoners appearing daily before that court. The holding cells were designed to deal with thirty-five prisoners at any one sitting. By 1973 seventy-five prisoners were appearing in the court each day. Subsequently, there were two or three escape bids here per week. Without any forward planning most ended in failure.

Among those who did succeed in escaping was a Loyalist prisoner named Sam Tweed. He made his dash for freedom in May 1974. A bomb scare was the apparent signal to put the bid into motion. As everyone was evacuating the Courthouse, several youths were seen to close in on his guards. Tweed was able to run out of the court while the guards were obstructed by youths who had apparently been standing in the foyer of the Courthouse.

In September 1974, four men got out through a window at Townhall Street police barracks where they were being held before their court appearance. They had successfully got up onto the roof before being recaptured. When charged with attempting to escape they claimed that they were merely protesting at conditions inside the prison when they were arrested. Before long another group of men saw a similar opportunity.

On 19 May 1975, five men connected with the IRSP escaped from Townhall Street. Harry Flynn, Vinty Fegan, Phil McDonnell, Billy Basset and Henry Doherty had been locked up in a holding cell at the courts in Chichester Street. A mixture of builders and labourers, they all were familiar with how a building was constructed. Looking for their chance to escape, they immediately noticed a flaw in the design of the skylight of their cell. The ceiling had been constructed of solid glass bricks set into a frame. In the cell itself it didn't take long to pull the boards off the benches. With one of these boards they prized open the glass slab. Hauling themselves through the opening, all of the men gained access to the roof. After dropping down into the adjacent Fire Station they made off into into the nearby Markets area. Once again the prison authorities were left with egg on their faces. Only one man was left in the cell when it was opened. He was charged with escaping but at his trial the judge discounted police evidence that he had been seen on the roof of the Courthouse. "He was in the cell when you closed the door and he was still in the cell when you opened the door again. How can I charge him with escape?"

It is only when one takes into consideration the amount of time and planning involved in the organisation and implementation of an escape operation, then the amount of escapes which had taken place purely because of luck, can be put into perspective. To say that they were amateurish breaks of luck, or that they were mindless acts by people who did not fully appreciate the risks involved, would be an improper assumption. Most of these lucky escapes were effected by people who had shown their determination to escape on previous occasions.

They also had to ensure that they could safely get away from their captors. Escaping from the building, be it a prison, a courthouse, or a hospital, is really only the first stage of any escape. For an escape to be a complete success the escapee not only has to break out but has also to succesfully evade recapture.

Aerial view of Long Kesh showing 'Silver City' in the foreground.

16. Clinical Assessments

1919 witnessed a hunger strike at Limerick Prison by prisoners in protest at being treated as ordinary criminals. The protesters were demanding the right to be treated as political prisoners. Their campaign of disobedience reached a climax when several of the men embarked on a hunger strike. After three weeks, one prisoner, Bobby Byrne was transferred to Limerick Union Hospital. He was held in a public ward with a constant guard of six RIC men by his bedside.

The Limerick IRA immediately put a rescue plan into operation. After studying the layout of the ward in which Byrne was being held they quickly decided on a plan of action. Sunday 6 April, 1919, was a quiet day and this fact meant that there would be a better chance of overpowering the guards. There were only two in the ward on a Sunday, Constables O'Brien and Spillane. There were others also on guard duty but they walked about the corridor. The IRA planned to make their move at visiting time and around twenty four men entered the ward, dispersing into pairs at different patients' beds. All but one of the rescue party was unarmed. At precisely three o'clock, the shrill blast of a whistle signalled the men to make their move. Outside the hospital a mourning coach was pulling into the courtyard in front of the hospital ready to whisk the hunger striker away to freedom.

The rescue team was aware that the RIC had orders to shoot their prisoner if any rescue attempt was made, so speed was important. The guards knew immediately what was afoot once the whistle was blown and as the IRA men moved in on them the RIC men produced their revolvers. A scuffle then ensued and as shots rang out other visitors in the ward dived for cover. Pandemonium broke out with yelling, screaming, and the sight of grown men wrestling on the ground in a corner of the ward. Both RIC men were shot and Bobby Byrne was helped from the bed. An overcoat was thrown around him and he was helped down the stairs and out of the hospital by two of the rescue party. The mourning coach was nowhere to be seen. It had gone to another doorway, and because of the urgency to get away from the scene, the two rescuers flagged down a pony and trap and at once headed for a safe house at Knocklisheen, three miles away. It was then that they realised to their horror that Byrne had been critically wounded, having been shot above the heart. His condition deteriorated rapidly and he was dead by 8.30pm. The RIC man, Constable O'Brien died later that day in hospital and Constable Spillane, the man who shot Byrne, survived in spite of the fact that he was seriously injured.

Escapes from hospitals continued right down to the present day. The most recent attempt was by Michael Bennett from Belfast's Lenadoon area who had been receiving treatment in the City Hospital for a bullet wound which he had received at the time of his arrest. He was caught as he tried to climb through a window at the hospital on 15 November 1995. In some instances prisoners deliberately created the situation where they would be so ill that they would have to be removed to hospital and then, once out of the stricter security regime at the prison they could easily escape. Not every escape had been so well planned however and happened just as the opportunity arose.

In June 1972, a hunger strike started at Crumlin Road jail. The strike was led by Belfast IRA man, Billy McKee, demanding political staus, akin to that which was enjoyed by internees, and the demand was that sentenced political prisoners be treated likewise. This hunger strike in itself led to another escape. Unlike the debacle of the 1919 hunger strike no one died, but one of the hunger strikers, Bobby Campbell, from Belfast's New Lodge area, got away after he was taken to the Mater Hospital, in Belfast.

Rescue attempts at hospitals have sometimes been surrounded in mystery and at other times they have led to the rescuers themselves being arrested and imprisoned. In the Fifties an apparent attempt was made to rescue Paul Murphy from St Bricin's Military Hospital. He had been removed from Mountjoy following an attempted breakout on 13 April 1958. Murphy had been suffering from acute appendicitis and was rushed to hospital as the other men were transferred to the Curragh. While at the hospital he was held under the constant guard of an NCO armed with a machine gun and three other soldiers armed with rifles.

On 12 May 1958, a man telephoned the Dublin Ambulance Service to come to St Bricin's to remove Paul Murphy from the military hospital. The porter asked where he was to be taken and was told by the 'doctor' that he would receive further instructions once he arrived. Once the ambulance crew arrived they were told to wait. After an hour had elapsed they were told that Murphy had already been transferred back to prison. It soon became apparent that a rescue bid had been abandoned due to unforeseen circumstances. The IRA issued a statement denying they had been involved in any rescue bid and it soon became rumoured that another

Republican group, named Saor Éire was behind the plot.

Many of those to escape were being treated in 'outside' hospitals for bullet wounds received during their arrests. This was the government's downfall. The hospitals within the prisons only provided basic recovery facilities and had no provision made within them for surgery or for any complicated medical attention. On these occasions the prisoners had to be moved to an 'outside' hospital under armed escort. Because of the civilian population who are also treated on the same premises as the prisoner, it was not becoming for the guards, such as British soldiers and RUC men, to go about brandishing loaded weapons. Any prisoner who found himself in such a situation soon realised that his guards would be severely restricted in opening fire within the wards and corridors of a civilian hospital. It was with this thought in mind that the inspiration for most of the hospital escape bids came to pass. By the time the Seventies arrived the newest batch of political prisoners had many chances for hospital rescues.

One such incident involved Gerry Fitzgerald who had been shot by the British army during a gun battle in Ballymurphy. On 16 July 1971, he was receiving treatment for his gunshot wounds at the Royal Victoria Hospital at Belfast. His guard consisted of two armed RUC men who were to watch over him day and night. Four men disguised as 'doctors' approached the guards and disarmed them. One of the men put Fitzgerald over his shoulder and headed off into the morning mists.

Early in 1972, Frank Quigley from Belfast, arrived at Musgrave Park Hospital having been shot in the leg by British soldiers at the time of his arrest. He was treated and remanded to Armagh Prison. On this first visit to the hospital Quigley realised that an escape could be pulled off but when he put the bones of his plans to the escape committee, they were against the idea. There was a possibilty that it could be successful and so the plan went ahead.

Several weeks later Quigley was returned to the hospital to have a caliper fitted. The ward in which he was being held was in the military wing on the first floor of Musgrave Park Hospital. There were other prisoners on the same floor but they were being treated in a different ward. The other patients were still too weak to walk about and Quigley used to visit to the ward to have a yarn or a game of chess with them.

British soldiers were in the ward constantly but there was never any aggravation. The atmosphere was the same as in any other hospital ward and the men just bided their time there until they would be strong enough to be returned to the Cages at Long Kesh. Jim Mulvenna, from the Bone, was one of the patients. He had been badly shot up — having been hit nine times during a gunbattle between the British

Army and the IRA at Ligoneil Mill on 13 February 1972. Casual conversation with an SAS captain at the hospital confirmed their belief that to escape down through the hospital and out the front doors would be fraught with difficulty. Instead, they opted to go out through the window of the ward on which Mulvenna and the other men were recuperating and go across fields towards the main road.

Before long the men got their hands on a hacksaw blade. They were faced with the difficulty of trying to cut the bars with the soldiers constantly sitting in the ward with them. To add to the problem, Quigley was the only man who was fit enough to do the work. Nevertheless, they proceeded with their plans at every opportunity. At times they cut the bars whilst supposedly playing chess by the window. Quigley was able to reach his arm behind the curtain to saw the bars while the soldiers thought they were innocently playing a chess game. On another occasion the men in the ward had a sing song while another bar was sawn through. The men were unaware that in Belfast and Derry the British Army had suffered heavy casualties that day. The Commanding Officer came into the ward to reprimand the men for their inconsiderate behaviour explaining that Musgrave was a hospital and that Republican prisoners there had been cared for regardless of their political persuasions. The men apologised for their behaviour — the Commanding Officer not realising the real reason for the noise that day.

Eventually the day came to go out (17 April), but there were problems at the last minute. The transport which had been arranged to pick them up waited around for a while but before long had departed without the prisoners. The following night Frank Quigley and Jim Mulvenna made their last minute preparations. Quigley tucked the dummy into his bed and made his way down the corridor to Mulvenna's ward. Quigley lifted out the large window from its frame. They then tied the rope, made from bed linen, to the remaining bars and let themselves down to the ground below, being careful not to arouse the Brits in the downstairs room. Mulvenna was very weak and the climb alone sapped most of his strength but they both made off across the hospital grounds to the perimeter faence. Scaling this fence they were inside a park. It was around 2.00am. Mulvenna was still dressed in his pyjamas but Quigley, dressed in civilian clothes but barefooted, decided that he would head towards the main road and from there make his way to the Falls where he would send back help for Mulvenna.

Mulvenna hid in the bushes while Quigley did as arranged. Before long Quigley got a lift to the Grosvenor Road from where he made his way to a relative's house. A rescue team made their way back to the area around Musgrave but could not locate Mulvenna. It later transpired that he had been picked up as he made his way over the M1 towards the graveyard. He was back in custody and was not released until 1976. On 20 June 1978, he was shot dead after being ambushed by the SAS at Ardoyne Loney.

The outside hospital appeared to be the place from where one could easily escape, if the opportunity either presented itself, or could be manipulated. Joe McKee escaped from the Royal Victoria Hospital on Sunday, 11 August 1973, under a different ruse. Forty-eight hours after having an appendectomy he walked into the toilets where a domestic's uniform had been strategically placed. McKee donned the uniform and calmly walked out of the hospital past his guard and into a female ward. From there he entered the main corridor and escaped out onto the Grosvenor Road.

In September 1973, Billy McAllister was being escorted to have a bath in the hospital. As he was being led along a corridor he fled the RVH in his pyjamas. British soldiers chased after him, out onto the Grosvenor Road, but McAllister evaded capture. The British Army sealed off the immediate area and conducted house to house searches to recapture him, to no avail.

Similar attempts which were successful were made by James Brown in 1972, Eamonn Campbell in 1973. Other hospitals which were the scene of escapes were the Lagan Valley Hospital at Lisburn, and the Curragh Military Hospital from where Sean McGettigan and Eamonn O'Sullivan escaped in August 1975.

The idea that it was possible to escape from a hospital was in the back of most prisoners' minds. Others back at the Cages in Long Kesh developed the theory even further. Why not try to escape from the hospital which was inside the prison camp itself? There were problems to overcome but as the prisoners proved, nothing is insurmountable. One group of men went on to prove just how easy it could be if the opportunities and luck could chance to happen at the same time.

On 26 September 1973, six men were caught after four of them had actually broken free from the prison complex. Five were from Belfast, Paddy Donnelly and John McMullan from the Lower Falls, Gerard Burns and Joseph Barnes from the Bone and Hugh Gerard McComb from the Short Strand. The other man was Patrick Joseph Doherty from Derry. They had taken over the hospital block at the Maze and after trussing the warders and made their escape on foot dressed in their captors' uniforms. John McMullan who was on the escape recalls what actually happened;

"Dinner time between 12.00am and 2.00pm was when you had your changeover where you had warders moving down into what they called 'their area' in the camp. They would have been going down and out through the Tally Lodge. Warders would have been going back and forth, in large numbers, changing shifts. Everybody was locked up during this time. It was a quiet period when there was supposed to be no movement throughout the camp but we noticed that when more than five men were going to the prison doctor, who was based in the hospital, that they were calling the doctor's lists late. This meant that those who were called stayed at the hospital compound instead of being brought back to their own cage during the 'no movement' period.

"To get to the hospital, you had to travel down from our Cage. We were in Cage 17 at this time, and I would say it was about a quarter of a mile to the prison hospital itself. The van used to come and pick us up so we decided that if we got about six of us to go to the doctor together there would be a possibility that we could pull a move here. We guessed that if they came up to our Cage, between 12.00am and 2.00pm we would be in that quiet period which would give us about an hour to an hour and a half to actually cover our tracks and make good an escape.

"We then watched the movements of the van and timed it. The van was arriving at our Cage at around 11.30am or 12.00am every day. We then began to put our plan into action. We had a couple of people who were good at woodwork and they made three 'shortarms'. They were a really good job. They cocked and everything else. If you had flashed them at anyone they would have taken them for the real thing. We had a couple of dry runs first of all. We put six names down all the time and it paid off. They took six at a time in the van and took us down to the hospital where we remained until after the 'no movement' period was over and the screws came back on duty.

"Next we had to calculate how many warders would be at the hospital itself. Any time we went into the hospital, there was one doctor and maybe one or two MOs (Medical Officers) and a PO (Principal Officer). There were also sick prisoners recuperating in the wards themselves. At the most we were reckoning on probably four people, maybe five at the most, who would stand in our way. We decided to make our move and take over the hospital. We told our contact on the 'outside' what the score was and they arranged to have transport for us. There would be two cars waiting with the keys under the front wheels and we knew exactly where to go to get them.

"We also had to be careful that there was no change of atmosphere in the Cage, for the warders would sense right away that something was going on. We kept the plans as tight as we could between the six of us, the OC (Officer in Command) and the IO (Intelligence Officer) of the Cage. They were the only people who would have known. We just kept it on a need to know basis. Nobody else had a clue what was going to happen that day. When it came about, as you can appreciate, every one of us was 'up to a hundred', waiting on the van. We were watching out the window when the van pulled up outside the small gate-house. The screw called out all the names and we filed out and into the back of the van. I remember us looking at each other and saying to ourselves that if we were lucky, maybe in few hours we would all be out. They didn't search you going to the hospital because it wasn't classed as going 'out of bounds'. We had the guns down our trousers as the van drove off. We were slagging and joking as we went, but all of us were aware of what we had to do.

"Since I was the first one out, I was to be called first. One warder was in charge of all six of us. He had all our security books which had all the details of our movements in and out of the cage which he had to have signed. So we got out of the van and the warder let us in through the airlock and closed the gate behind us. We entered the corridor of the hospital. The administration building was designed with a corridor and branching off this were surgeries, a doctor's room and various other offices. I was called first and I had the gun tucked down the waistband of my trousers. My job was to take the doctor, and whoever else was in the room, hostage.

"I pretended to the doctor, who was sitting at his desk in front of me, that I had a terrible pain in my stomach. I knew he would not be much of a problem to convince, but the MO who was there was 'a different kettle of fish'. He was a bit 'cocky on it', so I knew that I had to make the best impression on him from the outset. The doctor told me to get up on the bench behind him so that he could examine me. As I was going round behind him I took him in an arm-lock from behind. I had the gun to his head in an instant. I told him that we were taking over the hospital. At that the MO intervened. I told him that if he did what he was told the doctor would not get hurt. The MO did not think the gun was real but after I assured him that one wrong move and he would be fully accountable for the doctor's death, he panicked. Once I had convinced him that it was for real, I told him to start taking his clothes off. He had his uniform on underneath his white apron. Once he was undressed, I knocked the door and the rest of the lads, who had been standing outside, came in.

"Two of the men then went down the corridor and took the rest of the warders in the building, hostage. They were surprised to find three other MOs and a young 'crim' who was doing orderly duties at the hospital along with another doctor. In the meantime the others who were in the room with me helped to secure the doctor with surgical tape. The doctor was an elderly man so we did not tape him too tightly. I didn't think he was going to be much of a threat.

"In the meantime another one of us, dressed now in a warder's uniform, went out and called on the warder who was guarding the entrance gate. We told him that someone wanted him inside the hospital. Once he entered the building he too was taken hostage. We now had control of the hospital block. All the warders were stripped of their uniforms, taped with surgical tape and made to lie face down in one of the surgeries. Just when we thought we had it 'sussed', a knock came to the gate and two warders were at the other side. We took them in and tied them up. I think in the end we had about twelve or thirteen people tied up altogether. The phones were going as well and we had to make sure no one raised any alarm. Burns took the place of the guard who was on the gate. As he was standing there a warder walked down the road, going on duty. He asked him where the other warder was and Burns told him that he had just received a phone call from his wife and had to go on. He went on down the road, believing the story.

"We prepared to set off towards the Tally Lodge dressed as warders. I paired off with Paddy Donnelly. We were the first ones to go out. Joe Barnes and Paddy Doherty were next and Gerard Burns and Hokey McComb were last. The main road through the camp went past the Cages and you could see the men walking around, unaware that we were escaping. As we walked down the road we had to pass Cages 9, 10, 11, 12, and 13. Between every two cages there was a check. A warder would have been there checking passes and carrying out different security procedures. We went through every one of them and were never asked to produce anything. We reached Cage 6, where the internees were held, and where there was also a big gate. The only thing we were worried about by that stage was walking into Dáithí Fada who was a Security Officer by this stage, having progressed through the ranks since our imprisonment. He had been our Class Officer from Crumlin Road jail and had risen through the ranks of the Prison Service while we had been in custody. He mustn't have been on that day.

"To get to the Tally Lodge from here you had to pass through a wicket gate. We went up to this gate and the warder opened it. We continued to dander along, until we came to a catwalk which took you directly to the Tally Lodge itself. I saw all the warders queuing up at the Tally Lodge to get out but there was a gate beside them lying wide open so we walked towards it and walked straight out. We looked behind us and not one of the warders took us under their notice. We said to ourselves, 'Jesus what are we going to do now? We're out.' The next thing we saw were Saracen Personnel Carriers driving by. We were in fact inside the army camp which was directly outside the prison complex. Outside the Tally Lodge itself was a disused tank.

"We knew that we were not too far away from the actual road. There weren't any big walls, or anything, around the place and soldiers and various other personnel were wandering about the place. We still had the warders' uniforms on us and so we carried on as normal. We knew that the next pair of prisoners would be coming down behind us in about twenty minutes so we had to get out of the army camp and out of the area as quickly as possible.

"At that time a lot of the warders were what we used to call, 'bounty hunters' and they lived in a place in the camp which was known to us as 'Silver City'. 'Silver City' comprised of portacabin accommodation where these warders stayed night and day only going home every couple of months. When we went in through Silver City the place was deserted. We spotted this toilet. There was a wee lad there, he must have been a 'crim' whose duty must have been to clean in and around the warders' living quarters. Both of us went into these toilets and took the uniforms off. We left them in the cistern. We had our own clothes on underneath. You should have seen his face when we came back out again!

"From there we just wandered about the army camp looking for an opportunity to get through the wire. We came upon part of the camp where they were fixing Saracens and Jeeps. There wasn't much activity here and we headed towards a couple of buildings which appeared to be derelict. Going around the side of these buildings we saw the perimeter fences of the camp. There were two fences about ten feet high with a bit of barbed wire strung along the top. It was about 12.15pm at this stage and broad daylight. I climbed over first and just as I was doing so, I noticed a sentry post about twenty yards away, with a Brit in it. He never even noticed us. The gap between the fences was about ten feet and it was covered in coils of barbed wire. We clawed our way through this until we reached the second fence. The whole time we were waiting on the sentry opening fire. As I jumped down there was a ditch on the other side of it and I landed in the undergrowth. We had made it, we were out. Paddy Donnelly however got stuck on the wire so I went back to help him down. Just at that minute the alarms, horns, sirens, everything went off. We jumped down into the undergrowth. We knew that the warders, Brits and peelers had a set procedure to seal off all the roads simultaneously. We knew there was no use in trying to move from where we were because we would be easily spotted. We decided to dig in and hoped to move off under cover of darkness.

"After about fifteen or twenty minutes we could hear the search parties passing to and fro not too far from us. After about a half hour a dog went past. So, when it went on past we thought we had made it. Unfortunately it returned and before we knew it the Brits had their rifles trained on us. They frog-marched us up onto the road where they made us lie face down. They then searched us and tied our wrists behind our backs with plastic handcuffs and brought us back into the jail.

"The second pair to head down the road were also allowed through the different gates until they too reached the Tally Lodge. Unlike myself and Donnelly, they did not notice the wicket gate which they had been told about in the planning of the escape and so they carried on into the Tally Lodge, which was staffed by two army sergeants and some prison warders. Once inside they were asked to produce their tally chits. Barnes handed his over first. The warder studied it for a moment and then told Barnes that he had the wrong chit. Keeping his cool, Barnes bluffed the warder by saying that he was only new at the prison, having been brought down from Crumlin Road Prison the previous week. The two soldiers were non-plused at this excuse. Meanwhile the Tally Lodge began to fill up with other warders going off duty and it was therefore imperative that Barnes and Doherty got through the lodge security as quickly as possible. Thinking quickly, Barnes then suggested that as he was only going off for a cup of tea, perhaps he could have it sorted out for him when he came back again. The warder, realising that a queue was beginning to form inside the Tally Lodge agreed with this suggestion and Barnes and Doherty found themselves out at the gate of the prison but still inside the army base."

They had been told that there was a church inside this camp, behind which they could climb over the fence which would lead them out onto a road. This road led to a little hamlet at the prison gates. Parked in this village was a car with the keys sitting under the front mat. The two prisoners walked along the road looking for this church. On their path they met a British army colonel and they asked him for directions. Unfortunately the colonel did not know of the whereabouts of the church and the two prisoners walked about the camp looking for a suitable exit point. By the time they found a blind spot at the perimeter fence, three quarters of an hour had passed since they had left the hospital, so they knew that the last two prisoners, Burns and McComb would now be at the Tally Lodge. Just as they got through the fence the sirens went off. Some civilians saw the two of them as they ran across the road towards the village and before long soldiers were chasing after them. They were recaptured within five or ten minutes.

The last two prisoners had, in the meantime, left the hospital and made their way down to the Tally Lodge. Just as they reached the bottom of the road they noticed the warders running this way and that. Unperturbed, they continued on their way. Just at that, one warder approached them and asked them to produce their tally. As Burns reached to his pocket more warders arrived on the scene shouting that the prisoners were escaping having taken over the hospital. They were caught. It was back to the drawing board once again. One lesson which was learned by everyone, was that the prison was only as strong as its weakest link and they had discovered where that weakness lay. The prisoners had made unprecedented success with their plans even though their knowledge of the layout and security procedures in the camp were relativly sketchy. The core of their escape was one which was used time and time again.

Many of the mistakes which these men made showed how important planning and timing would be in effecting a successful breakout. The 'hospital team' were discovered when the alarm was raised shortly after the last two men left the hospital compound. Once they had left, it was not long before the hostages realised that their captors had left and that there was, in fact, no one watching over them. They quickly made their way to the alarm buttons. The escapees may have had limited success on this occasion but the lessons learned from it by Republican prisoners were to have embarassing repercussions in years to come.

Aerial view Magilligan showing the old compounds alongside the new H-Blocks.

17. The Great Pretenders.

The impostors' greatest asset was their ability to change their appearance. Switching places with someone while on a visit or taking someone's place on a bail release has also been a popular ploy down the years. Only some were successful however. One of the first people to use such a ruse was Peadar O'Donnell, author and social reformer from Donegal.

In 1924 he was imprisoned along with thousands of other men by the Free State government. He bluffed the guards and escaped from Harepark camp on the Curragh on 16 March 1924. His story was one which was copied many times. He left the accommodation hut at 3.00am in the morning dressed in a Free State soldier's uniform. He calmly strode up to the main gates (two altogether) and they were opened to him without any problems. He headed off on foot and soon found sanctuary at the house of a local Republican. Later, he went back and held rank on the IRA Army Executive and eventually the Army Council. Dressing as a soldier has also been a ploy which has been tried on numerous other occasions.

When the civil war broke out in Ireland the Free State authorities were inundated with prisoners. So many men and women had been taken prisoner that they were housed, not only in prisons and camps, but in military barracks and even police stations. It was inevitable that many prisoners would escape in the confusion. The ploy of disguise has been used from the earliest of times to fool the guard and it works on the basis that no matter how efficient a prison regime believes it is, it still depends on humans and therefore is prone to mistakes.

The prison visit was another opportunity for potential escapers. The prisoner would basically swap places with his or her visitor. The visitor sometimes would be escorted all the way back to the cell in his place and whenever he believed that the escapee had got far enough away he would then reveal his real identity. It has been used from earliest time. Even during the civil war it was used against the prison regimes of the new Free State government.

ESCAPE OF IRREGULAR FROM ENNISCORTHY BARRACKS

An Irregular named J J Nolan has, say, "Iris an Airm" escaped from custody in Enniscorthy under the following circumstances: On 23rd inst., his wife made an application to see the prisoner stating that she required an interview in connection with business matters. She stated that herself or her sister would seek admission about 8.30pm on that evening. Desiring to inconvenience her as little as possible, the request was granted by the OC of the Troops. About 8.30pm, Miss Cosgrave, Mrs Nolan's sister, presented herself for admission and was allowed into the barracks to visit the prisoner. She had concealed on her person, a second lady's costume, which she handed over to Nolan. In the cell a change was made as a result of which the prisoner passed through the guards similar to the visitor who called to see him, she remaining inside until he got away.

The OC of the area has now issued orders, in consequence of this violation of privilege, that prisoners will not be permitted to receive visitors in the barracks.

(Freemans Journal, 29 September 1922)

Inside the prisons this impersonation ploy has worked on several occasions. In the majority of cases the escapee is dependent on the warders or soldiers not being too well acquainted with the prisoner. Obviously, if the prisoner is a well known figure then it will be ultimately more difficult. Two fine examples of this were Gerry Dowdall's escape by this method on 12 December 1973 from Crumlin Road Jail and Jimmy Burns who escaped twenty four hours later when he switched places with his visitor in the visiting area of Long Kesh. In order to prevent such a security breech, the warders kept prisoners and their visitors apart. The story of prisons and prison camps are replete with such instances. Most of them failed miserably.

Men not only switched places on the visits but at every given opportunity. Sometimes prisoners would be released on their appeal. When they were returned from the court to their Cage, or cell, they would have been 'beaten up' or tied up to show that they had no part in the conspiracy. The switch would have been made and the escapee, masquerading as the prisoner, would then bluff his way through the various security checks and walk through the front gates. Some of these escape bids have been humorous failures. Once a release order was issued to the prisoner and he was told to prepare himself for release, he then said goodbye to the other prisoners. All of his personal belongings would have been sent out of the Cage to the reception area. On the morning of the release the prisoner was brought to the prison hospital to undergo a medical examination. Afterwards he was taken to the reception area of the hospital to have his identity checked and from there he was taken to collect his personal belongings and released. It was through these different procedures that the disguise was usually discovered.

The first man to successfully escape from Long Kesh masquerading as another prisoner named Jimmy Walsh, who had been ordered for release, was Ivor Bell. Bell was classified as the government's most prized prisoner, being one of the Republican movement's leaders in the North. He had previously been interned from 1956 to 1962 and was part of the ceasefire negotiations in London in 1972, between the Provisional IRA and the British Government. The British Government, therefore, heralded his arrest in February 1973, as a major coup against the IRA. The fact that Bell had only been in custody seven weeks when he escaped was a major source of embarrassment for the prison's security chiefs. Ivor Bell was rearrested on 28 May 1974.

Another well-known figure in the Republican movement at the time was Gerry Adams from Belfast. He tried to use the same ruse to fool the guards in July 1974. Ivor Bell, who by this stage had been recaptured, along with four others were charged with helping in the conspiracy which failed.

One such escape had been planned in advance. The OC of the hut along with the man who was supposed to change places with the potential escapee had made all the necessary preparations. The man who was due for release had bright red hair so a wig was smuggled in and the escapee was dressed to look like him. Their similarities were quite close although Gerard Burns, the potential escapee, did not feel too certain about it. In the huts some prisoners had curtained off the section around their bed for privacy and the OC and the escapee made all the final preparations. To test out their plan, they called someone up to the hut and when he went away someone else called him and asked him who was with the OC. He did not recognise Burns and thought it had been the other man. The release day eventually arrived and the warder came to the Cage and called the prisoner. Burns set off in his place. He believed that the screws had 'smelt a rat' from the minute he was between the gates because, he alleged, he could sense that their attitude had changed, although no- one said anything.

Burns recalls what happened;

"I was brought to the hospital and the doctor examined me. He asked me all the questions as to my health and so on. I answered everything without a hitch. Then the doctor told me to drop my trousers. He said he had to look at my privates. I knew then that there was something wrong but I had no choice. I dropped my trousers and underpants. He knew then that the hair down below was a different colour from the hair on my head. Then the screw who was present the whole time reached over and tugged the wig from my head. I started laughing. What could I do? I was caught. I was taken to the boards for a few days and then was returned to the Cage. About a year later I was brought to court and charged with the escape bid and got three years."

Disguise was something that most Republican prisoners could enact although some were better than it than others. Larry Marley was one person who became a master for disguise. He was a deft hand at making uniforms and other such accessories, with limited materials and resources. Marley was from the Ardoyne area in Belfast and had been imprisoned in the early 1970's He eventually ended up in the H-Blocks and was the mastermind behind the 1983 escape using the food lorry. His life within the prison system is an astonishing tale of intrigue. Constantly trying to invent new ways of escape he helped many prisoners find their freedom from the prison. By the time Larry arrived at the Cages of Long Kesh he had already got a reputation for his ingenious ploys at beating the system. Once at Long Kesh he quickly formed a group around him which did nothing else but plan escapes. He was able to gather some other master craftsmen to make uniforms and carve replica guns and in the scenes similar to those the public were seeing in films like 'The Great Escape', men's talents were coordinated by the Camp staff to effect a break out.

Larry's plan was to have a team of six men dress as an army foot patrol which was a regular feature of camp life. This team had watched the British soldiers who were employed as guards in the camp. Cage 16 was right beside the wire and the prisoners could see how the soldiers regularly changed duty. Before long this routine had been meticulously timed. It was noted that the soldiers in the watch-towers were equipped with GPMGs (General Purpose Machine-Guns) but the patrols carried short-arms. Having successfully tailored camouflage, the prisoners cut the wire and the six went off down the road. They were caught before they even reached the front gate and after a short stay on the boards, they were brought back to the Cage. All was not lost however. At their court appearance for this escape attempt the men were taken out to Newry Courthouse from where they did successfully escape. Larry Marley's run was short lived however and he was recaptured in Belfast in 1977 and sentenced to ten years for possession of weapons.

Marley's group was not the only one in the jail which was constantly conspiring, there were others. Each had their own ideas which were closely guarded from the other groups. They also had their own methods of sourcing materials which might be used in any such attempt. They worked independently, their only link being the camp staff, who had to sanction any such plans. Eventually some of the individuals involved in these groups realised that if they coordinated their plans by merging some of the groups then they would have a better chance of success. Three such men were Larry Marley, Brendan 'Bik' McFarlane and Pat McGeown. By and by they all ended up in Cage 12 where they were able to pool their resources. Things did not run smoothly from the outset, however, as all the men were wary of each other. They didn't want anyone else stealing their ideas. It took about three to four months before the committee gelled to such an extent that they were actually working as a team. There were a couple of minor attempts. They initially planned to tunnel out of the camp but the tunnel was discovered in January 1978. This resulted in the three being split up and dispersed through other Cages in the camp. Eventually they were brought together again. The use of disguise and adopting the routine of their captors, was, it was believed, the surest way to gain their freedom. Pat McGeown, one of those involved in one such escape explains how the plan developed;

"We had been debating the idea of the three of us going out dressed as screws. We had good information about the security procedures at the front gate. We knew that in order to pass through the security check we had to have a metal tally disc which was handed over to collect the pass. We needed to know the layout of the jail at the kennels so we used a pet cat as a ploy to get out that far. The kennels were about three hundred yards from the Cage. Initially Larry went out as far as the hospital. Then, after a month or so he told the warder that he had to bring the cat over to the kennels. Gradually a pattern was emerging and the previously unmapped areas of the prison were gradually filled in. The main escape that the three men had planned was based on the cream of the intelligence gathered at the prison.

"We had to find a way of getting out of the Cage itself. This is where the wirecutters would come into operation. It was our intention to cut the wire at a blind spot and then step outside the Cage dressed as screws and blend in with the normal everyday routine at the jail. At that time there was a mixture of screws at the jail — the local screws were complimented by warders from Scotland, Wales and England and they all had different uniforms. We made the badges out of the toothpaste tubes and a tailor in the Cage stitched the rest of the uniform from various pieces of clothing which had been gathered together.

"We were fairly confident of overcoming any foreseeable problems which might arise between the Cage and the front gate. We were all set to go when word was sent in to us to postpone the escape until after the Easter holidays. Reluctantly we agreed, and so the plan was put on hold until about a week after Easter. The day before we were to go we cut the wire at the blind-spot. This was not as easy as it at first appeared. There was a certain amount of risk involved because it was part of prison security procedure to do a wire check. Each night a warder went along the wire, tapping it with his baton making sure it wasn't cut. The point where we had to cut the wire was at a blind-spot. There was a screw on watch at the top of the walkway watching this specific point. There was another Cage facing us across this walkway. During the build up to the escape we regularly asked the screw to pass records or books across to the other Cage, which the screw obliged in doing. On the night before we were talking through the wire to someone from the other Cage while we were cutting. We tied the hole up with the wire ties which used to be on the packaging from loaves of bread.

"The next morning everything went into motion. We had to change our appearance, so I had my previously long hair cut fairly short and neat. The others changed their appearances in a similar fashion. We went through the wire that afternoon at about 3.00pm. To get rid of the screw who was guarding the Cage we had someone call him down to the wire to hand some bird seed over to the other Cage. Just as he was about to reach up over the wire to receive it, it was pointed out to him that the bag was going to burst and perhaps it would be better if he went around to the gate at the front of the Cage where he could collect it with less chance of the bag splitting. He obliged and accordingly went off. This meant that he was, in effect, about fifty or sixty yards from the blind-spot. We went through the wire and went off in the opposite direction.

"What I had to do was go up to the Cage which was facing ours as though I was coming from elsewhere in the camp. I was to leave records in for another prisoner. Just as I got to the gate one of the regular screws from our Cage met me at the entrance. He looked at me and you could tell that he knew my face but he did not realise from where. Anyway, he was most obliging and told me he would leave them in for me and he let me go on my way. From there I headed for one of the gates in the main wall which led to what was called a 'sterile area', which is where the hospital was. When I arrived at the gate there were no checks and the gate was opened and closed after me. Larry and 'Bik' had passed through one of the other gates which was about two hundred yards away from me and I could see them in front of me. Just then I met an SO (Senior Officer). He was a Welshman and started talking to me. I told him that I was going off duty as my wife had just given birth and that I was going off to see her at the hospital. He decided to walk down with me. So here I was stuck with this screw as I headed for the front gate. As we were walking down the road I saw 'Bik' and Larry, who were still about two hundred yards in front of me, veering off to one side and knew immediately that something was wrong as this was not in the plan. The Welsh guy, meantime said 'congratulations' and that he'd probably see me later for a pint, he then headed off!

"I caught up with Larry and 'Bik' and they told me what had went wrong. There had been a change in the regular routine because of the Easter holidays and the metal tally discs had been replaced with a plastic card. We were now faced with a dilemma, either we could try and go back to the Cage or we could continue as planned. After much debate we decided to continue. Our initial plan was to get through this gate with our tally chits. This gate led to an area where the maintenance workshops were located. We had planned to take control of the workshop and then dress as tradesmen. We then would have went to the front gate on the pretence of fixing the lights on the outside.

"We could see that the screw who was checking the ID was on one side of the gate but that there were vehicles coming and going. It would have been possible to pass through the gate using the cover of one of these vehicles. As it happened me and Larry got through without a hitch but 'Bik' was unfortunately spotted. Once 'Bik' was spotted we knew the game was up so we loitered about until the rest of the screws arrived. We were taken to the boards. The eventual outcome of the escape was that we lost our status and received six months suspended sentences and ended up 'on the blanket' in the H-Blocks."

Some of the attempted breakouts that Larry Marley was noted for were clever feats of ingenuity that only failed because of bad timing and lack of sufficient information as to prison regimes and outlay. These problems and mistakes were quickly overcome when he, along with several other seasoned escape planners, pulled off the biggest escape in British prison history, when thirty eight men broke out of Long Kesh in 1983. Like Peadar O'Donnell, McBride and others before them, the Republican prisoners at Long Kesh learned quite quickly which weaknesses could be exploited for escape. The first successful escape from the camp was in February 1972, Francis McGuigan calmly walked through the gates disguised as a priest. Unbelievably, another escapee did exactly the same thing on 9 September 1973. Every Sunday a priest would come in and serve Mass for the men in Long Kesh. On this particular Sunday Rev Gerard Green was found tied up in the Cage where he had been celebrating Mass. His brother, John Francis Green meanwhile made good his escape. The ruse was used again by a man from the New Lodge area of Belfast named Pat Campbell. He also escaped dressed as a priest who had been celebrating Mass at the Cages on 20 July 1975.

The prisoners who were involved in these plots have proven to be the kernel which kept the system on its toes, so to speak. To them it mattered not one iota if they were serving twenty years or just two weeks they still refused to be subjugated by the prison system. The use of disguise has been just one way of doing this and the grand masquerade involved must deservedly classify these prisoners as the real pretenders.

Aerial view of the Maze prison complex.

18. Transportation.

Transportation can mean different things to different people. In bygone days transportation meant being exiled to penal settlements throughout the British Empire. With the demise of that empire however and the succesive escapes since that time transportation has come to have a slightly different meaning.

No prison is secure. There are weaknesses in every one of them. Most of these weaknesses are down to human error. With every escape, and escape bid, the prison designers have been able to build newer and more up-to-date top security prison complexes, where movement in and out has been whittled down to the bare minimum. It has been a constant game of cat and mouse, with both captors and prisoners continually reviewing procedures. One aspect where prison security has been compromised is where a routine has been established, one such routine being prison traffic. Vehicles have to go in and out of prison. Deliveries of food have to made. Refuse has to be collected. Ambulances have to gain access and the movement of other traffic begins to form a routine. At these points security is usually at its tightest. This fact has not gone unnoticed and has been exploited on many occasions in Irish prisons. A press release in the *Freeman's Journal* on 22 August 1921, revealed one such escape:

> *Mr James Staines who had been interned at Hare Camp, Curragh since March 1921, successfully escaped on Saturday, August 20 1921. Mr Staines was walking about in the company of other prisoners when, shortly before 3.00pm, two lorries containing quantities of timber and military supplies were driven into the camp. It is believed that their destination was intended to be the Rath Camp and, on discovering their mistake, the military drivers proceeded to rectify their mistake.*

When the lorries turned around Mr Staines and another prisoner, observing spaces in the main body of both lorries, suddenly made a dash forward and boarded them, one concealing himself in the first lorry and the other in the second.

The first lorry drove past the sentries who noticed nothing amiss. The concealed prisoner, when the danger zone had been passed, dropped cautiously to the ground and took cover. The lorry continued on to the Rath Camp, neither the driver nor the soldier sitting beside him being aware of what had happened. The presence of the prisoner on the second lorry was detected and he was immediately taken back to the custody of his guards. Mr Staines successfully evaded the guards and escaped.

When we examine the more recent escapes by Irish political prisoners it is clear how prison security could be compromised in this way and is indeed the reason why the prison authorities have subsequently tried to keep traffic in and out of the prisons to a minmium. One of the first men to avail of the facility of frequent motor traffic visiting the prison where he was being held, was Brendan Hughes from Belfast's Lower Falls. He escaped in a refuse truck which was leaving Long Kesh at Christmas 1973.

The refuse truck became a regular spot for escapees to make their bid. Even Sean McBride tried to escape this way in the 1920's but was caught. On 7 April 1973, two men, Niblock and Neill, escaped after hiding in the refuse trailer. They were caught several hours later, after a head count revealed that they were missing from the Cage which held Loyalist prisoners.

On 8 July 1974, Owen Coogan was watching intently for his moment to conceal himself on board a trailer which regularly arrived at his cage to collect rubbish. The trailer went around the camp pulled by a tractor. Successfully concealing himself on board, it left the camp and headed to the rubbish dump on the outskirts of Dromara where the rubbish was tipped out. Coogan remained hidden under the trailer until the British army escort pulled off. He immediately set off on foot, dressed as a jogger, towards Dromara town. He had a good headstart before it was noticed that he was missing. Recaptured by an RUC mobile patrol several hours later he was dressed in running shorts, vest and slippers. At his trial the following year Justice Gibson said he could understand that, as a detainee Coogan may have felt he had a duty to escape. This 'understanding' did not prevent the Judge handing down a further prison sentence for escaping from 'lawful custody'. Coogan was put behind the wire again, this time as a sentenced prisoner.

The failed attempts to escape from Long Kesh by this route gradually increased. Disaster struck in April of 1974 when a Republican detainee once again tried to escape by clinging to the underside of a refuse lorry. Following the escape attempt,

Mark Graham was transferred to hospital seriously ill. Graham's bid for freedom resulted in a search of the camp which led to a major riot as soldiers tried to conduct a headcount.

The most horrific injuries occurred when Loyalist prisoners again tried to get away by this method. On 9 August 1984, the anniversary of internment, two UDA members, Edward Pollock from Belfast and Benny Redfern from Desertmartin hid in a plastic refuge bin hoping to be brought to freedom by the refuge truck. When the bin was tipped into the back of the truck Refern was caught in the machinery and crushed to death. His screams alerted the warders and Pollock was arrested at the scene. Both men had been held at the Cages at the camp.

The H-Blocks were designed to be jails within jails. Control of movement was of the utmost importance. The government, who had been planning the new regime for prison management, had looked at different ways of fortifying security measures. They had been advised by various strategists and advisors such as Lord Gardiner not to reintroduce compound-type prisons and instead to revert back to cellular confinement. The government, faced with a rapidly increasing prison population was forced to construct temporary accommodation beside Long Kesh. This new accommodation was built according to the 'experts' advice' and was intended to contain the prison's rising population until a new top-security prison could be completed at Maghaberry. This temporary jail was called HMP 'Maze' Cellular although people continue to refer to the prison as Long Kesh.

The 'Maze' consisted of eight self-contained units called H-blocks. Each H-Block was a secure unit surrounded by a high steel fence and reels of razor wire. The prison designers copied, to a certain extent, the design of the old Victorian prison outlay, to enable the least amount of warders to guard a larger amount of prisoners. The units were shaped like the letter H and contained two sets of two Wings, each Wing containing twenty six cells. These Wings were connected by the centre piece of the H, which was known as 'the Circle', similar to the old prison complexes like Crumlin Road and Mountjoy. The Circle was the control centre for each block and it was here that the warders' mess room, toilets, control room and Governor's office were situated. Each wing was peppered with emergency alarm buttons and the control room of the circle was connected to a central control room which oversaw security throughout the prison.

Each of the eight Blocks were surrounded by a sixteen feet high fence. The entire prison was divided into segments, which were in turn divided by concrete walls and wire fences. There were no more than three H-blocks to each segment. The entire jail was surrounded by a two thousand yard concrete wall, beyond which was a wire fence of razor wire. Twelve watch towers on this perimeter wall, one every two hundred yards ensured there were armed sentries on guard twenty four hours a day. It was within such an enviroment that the biggest breakout in British prison history occurred. Some of those who had planned this escape had been involved in other breakouts. Many of them, having previously been held in the Cages, had benefitted from being classified as Special Category prisoners. This Special Category Status had been lost by most members of the escape committee after they were caught trying to breakout on an earlier occasion. Consequently, they found themselves reimprisoned in the H-Blocks at the Maze.

Many reports were compiled to advise the government in formulating prison strategy. One of the most important was that compiled by Lord Gardiner. In what was to become known as 'the criminalisation policy', Lord Gardiner's report recommended the withdrawal of Special Category Status for political prisoners. Coupled with the use of the Diplock court system, it was decided that any prisoners convicted after March 1976 would be treated as ordinary criminals. All prisoners would do prison work and wear prison uniforms and would integrate fully regardless of political or religious persuasion in the new cellular accommodation. This move by the government was rigourously opposed by most political prisoners.

Those prisoners who joined the protest lost remission on their sentences and as the protests escalated, a hunger strike was embarked upon. Ten men eventually died before the government was forced to conceed most of the prisoners' demands. The inmates did not win everything straight away, however, once the protests ended the prisoners' movements became less restricted within the jail. Since most of those inside were political prisoners it did not take long before they had a majority in every block. To prevent any disorder and possible deaths whilst in custody prisoners were segregated according to their political affiliation.

Those who had constantly dreamt of freedom before the Hunger Strikes and the ending of Political Status, began to gain a general knowledge of the prison layout. Before long the old ideas came streaming back, until eventually the IRA inside the jail realised their potential. The government authorities, who controlled the new H-Blocks, fervently believed that this was 'the most secure prison in Europe'.

Sir James Hennessy pointed out that, *no prison is ever more secure than the weakest member of its staff.... absolute security can never be guaranteed without resort to inhuman and unacceptable methods.*

Republican prisoners had, for a long time, realised that this was the case. While the Blanket protest was continuing at the prison, the prisoners were locked in their cells twenty four hours per day. They did not get out to use the toilet or washing facilities and were served meals in their cells. The only time movement took place was during wing shifts, visits or on Sundays when they were brought into the canteen to hear Mass. Not only that, but the prisoners were naked. The ending of the protests and the hunger strikes changed this arrangement. The changeover to a new relaxed regime was almost instant. Prisoners began to agree to do vocational work which gave them access to the workshops and gardens outside the H-Blocks themselves but still within the complex. What were previously unmapped grounds began to become familiar as prisoners could get a proper bearing of everything. Very soon a detailed picture of the layout of the entire prison was built up.

The importance of traffic coming in and out of the jail had featured prominently in the minds of political prisoners down through the years. Escapes this way had always been limited to one or two men at a time but by 1983 the planners were thinking of mass escapes using the same idea. This, combined with what they had learned from previous successful and attempted escapes went to help the prisoners amass a wealth of experience. H7 at the time held those who were serving extremely long sentences. The block also contained some of the IRA's most experienced operators. Before long, an escape committee inside the prison began to organise a breakout involving these men. If successful, this would prove to be, not only the biggest escape in the history of the State of Northern Ireland, but also the biggest IRA operation ever mounted in the North since the founding of the State in 1922.

This time they planned to use a Bedford lorry which regularly drove around the prison. This lorry would be capable of transporting up to forty men at a time. It was covered in and was used to deliver the ready-cooked food canisters to each block. The same lorry, driver and helper delivered to all the Blocks on the same day and the complete operation took around an hour and a half to complete. The planners were watching and timing its every move. They also knew that the food lorry was never searched even though it had to go through several gates as it travelled around the prison.

The food lorry was large enough to take all those who wanted to go from H7. There were thirty eight men chosen to go out, the majority of them serving long prison terms. The escape would be in three distinct stages. Firstly, control of the 'circle' area and the control room had to be secured. Secondly, the food lorry had to be driven out of the prison after the Tally Lodge had been secured. Thirdly, the rearguard in the jail had to ensure that the warders did not set the alarms off too soon and that a fifty strong IRA unit were to be in place at a rendezvous point ten miles outside the prison to ensure the complete successful getaway of the escapees.

Of the remaining men who were to be left behind at H7, a rearguard was chosen to ensure that the warders remained tied up and that none of them could raise the alarm before the lorry had made a good getaway. Everyone who was to take part in the escape plan was briefed by Bobby Storey and Brendan McFarlane prior to the day of the planned operation. Weapons were smuggled in and those chosen to use them, if necessary, were carefully selected. There were five small firearms smuggled into the prison shortly before the escape operation was to start.

Sunday was a quiet day at the prison. All the men would be confined to the Block because there were no visits or prison work and there were less screws on duty. Mass was held that day at 'C' Wing. Dinner was served at 12.00am. At 12.30pm everyone was locked in their cells. The prisoners were unlocked at 2.05pm and those involved took up their positions. Seven men, Bobby Storey, Brendan McFarlane, Gerry Kelly, Brendy Mead, Tony McAllister, Rab Kerr and Sean McGlinchey were working in the Block as orderlies. All of these men were armed and it was their job to securely take over the circle area.

The signal for the operation to go into motion began with McFarlane calling down to 'A' and 'B' Wings for a "bumper". This was the electric floor polisher which the orderlies used to polish the floors of the block. At this signal everyone moved together and within a matter of seconds every warder on duty that day had been overpowered.

The most important place inside each Block was the control room. John Adams, the warder assigned for duty that day was in his position as usual when Gerry Kelly produced a gun and told him to do as he was told. At that minute the toilet door, to the right of the control room door, opened and a warder came strolling out, oblivious to what was happening in the circle. Kelly's attention was temporarily diverted. Adams tried to slam the control room door shut. Kelly was able to put his arm round the door where he fired at Adams. Two shots were fired and the warder lay slumped behind the door. He had been shot in the eye. The shots echoed through the Block. McFarlane meanwhile took a brush and headed out towards the front gate where another warder was on sentry duty. He quickly overpowered him and brought him back into the Block.

The Block was now completely under the control of the IRA. Now all that had to happen was to sit tight and wait for the lorry to deliver the food to them. The Happy Wagon was what the lorry had been nicknamed through the years. Now it was as though this nickname had taken on a new meaning.

Inside H7, the warders were corralled into the classroom. They were stripped of their uniforms, hooded and tied together. The uniforms were donned by the prisoners. Those whose job it would be to take the Tally Lodge and the front gate would be disguised as prison warders.

The lorry arrived at 3.30pm and was allowed to enter the Block. The unsuspecting driver (a prison warder) was taken from the lorry and brought into the the the medical room where he was put through a psychological briefing by those who were in command of the escape He was assured that providing he did exactly as he was told, he would come to no harm. It was explained to him that there was an escape taking place and that he was going to drive the lorry out through the main gate. He was told that he was going to be tied to the seat in the cab and that a grenade would be placed under him. One of the escapees, who would be armed, would keep him in his sights at all times. Everyone then got into the lorry - thirty eight men in total. The last men into the lorry were those who were dressed as warders. They would be the ones who were getting out first.

The lorry headed off out of the block. Everyone was ordered to be quiet. Before long they reached the first gate and as planned were waved through. The same thing happened with the second gate. There was only one last gate to go through. This was the main gate at the Tally Lodge. Once the lorry stopped those who had been dressed as warders jumped out of the back. They all knew precisely where they had to go and what they had to do. Everything at this stage was going to plan.

The lorry had pulled up outside the Tally Lodge. Inside this building was like the valve through which staff entered and left the prison. Everyone, including warders were to produce identification and were frisked before they were allowed entry. The escape was running behind time because of the late arrival of the food lorry. The helper was taken from the cab of the lorry and led into the Lodge.

James Ferris was on duty inside. It was his job to search warders as they came on duty. After being searched and changing his pass, another warder carried on through the Lodge and out the gate at the other end. He was at once held up by Bobby Storey, who brought him back into the Tally Lodge and placed him in the transport office. Another warder was on duty at the inner gate of the Lodge. He too was taken hostage. One warder was in the search area when another escapee took him hostage at gunpoint. Gerry Kelly watched over the prisoners while the warder who was in the search area was forced to answer the telephones.

James Ferris immediately started to shout when he was confronted by the escapees. He tried to alert the other warders. As he ran out of the Tally Lodge he was stabbed. He was overpowered and brought back to join the others in the transport office. The shift change, meanwhile, was just beginning and just as the prisoners were beginning to get control of the Tally Lodge, large numbers of warders began to arrive for duty. As they came to the gate they were taken hostage and led in to the room to join the others. Before the escpaees knew what was happening up to forty warders were being held at gunpoint with more arriving as each second passed.

Eventually one of the warders coming through the gate recognised Brendan McFarlane, who was 'on duty' outside the Tally Lodge. This warder, after alerting the other warders in his vicinity, made a run for McFarlane. He tried to raise the alarm by blowing his whistle. McFarlane retreated inside the Tally Lodge to alert the others. Just at that moment the other warders started struggling with Bobby Storey, who dropped his weapon in the fracas. Confusion then ensued. Everything was happening very quickly. Storey managed to get to the others, who were still awaiting further orders in the back of the lorry. By this stage they knew something had gone wrong. Storey pulled open the shutter and said, "the ball's busted. Everybody out." Any warders who had thought only a few men had escaped soon realised the enormity of the escape operation as man after man scrambled from the lorry. All hell broke loose as a free-for-all erupted between the prisoners and the warders. A few seconds before this, the British soldiers in the lookout towers watched in quiet amusement at what they thought were warders fighting among themselves on the ground below. With the emergence of the prisoners from the back of the lorry they very quickly realised what was afoot. Men ran in different directions in a last desperate bid to gain their freedom. Robert Kerr, Denis Cummings and Edward O'Connor held most of the warders back as the majority of men headed for the wire. As this was happening, the sirens, indicating a major security alert was under way, began to wail and the British soldiers began to open fire.

Several prisoners, warders and escapees had been either shot, stabbed or beaten up. Several other prisoners, who had been left behind at H7 were later awarded substantial sums of money by way of compensation for injuries received as the RUC and prison staff took their revenge for the escape.

One man, James Ferris, a prison warder, died during the escape. According to the State Pathologist for Northern Ireland, it was his belief that Ferris had died of *acute coronary insufficiency due to coronary atheroma and emotional stress.* It was revealed at the inquest that Ferris had not been in good health having suffered several previous heart attacks but that *in an otherwise healthy individual they (the stab wounds) should not have caused serious incapacity or death.*

Of the thirty eight men who had escaped nineteen were recaptured immediately afterwards. Twenty-nine of the escapers ran towards the barbed wire fence. Twenty-seven made it over the top of the hill, down a thirty foot gulley and up the other side. For some this was to be their only taste of freedom. Six escapees drove down from the Tally Lodge to the main entrance gate in a warder's car, where, after jamming it between the open gates some of them got away on foot. Eddie O'Connor, Denis Cummings and Rab Kerr were arrested almost immediately at the

Tally Lodge; Jimmy Donnelly and Jim 'Jaz' McCann were arrested as the car they were escaping in stopped at the front gates. Billy Gorman was caught after he was ensnared in the wire and Harry Murray was arrested after he was shot by British soldiers while trying to free Gorman; Bobby Storey, Sean McGlinchey, Peter Hamilton and Joe Simpson were arrested about half an hour after the escape, while hiding in the River Lagan; Jimmy Burns was arrested about twenty minutes after the escape at an RUC checkpoint; Marcus Murray and Martin McManus were arrested when they were stopped on the A2 in a Mercedes; Gary Roberts was arrested later that same night as he crossed a field; Paul Kane and Brendan Mead were arrested outside Castlewellan the following day; Patrick McIntyre and Joe Corey were arrested forty eight hours later near Castlewellan.

Of the other nineteen men Robert Russell was recaptured in Dublin, 26 May 1984; Kieran Fleming died following an engagement with the SAS in Fermanagh, 2 December 1984; Jim Clark was recaptured near Pettigo, 3 December 1984; Gerry McDonnell was recaptured at Glasgow, 22 June 1985; Brendan McFarlane and Gerry Kelly were both recaptured in Holland, January 1986; Seamas McIlwaine was ambushed and killed by the SAS at Roslea, County Fermanagh, 26 April 1986; Pádraic McKearney was ambushed and killed by the SAS at Loughall, County Armagh, 8 May 1987; Seamus Clarke and Tony Kelly were both recaptured in Dublin, 26 November 1987; Dermot Finucane was recaptured at Granard, County Longford, November 1987; Kevin Barry Artt and Jim Smith were both recaptured in USA, 3 June 1992; and Paul Brennan was recaptured in USA, 21 January 1993. Terence Kirby was recaptured in USA in February 1994.

The others, Seamas Campbell, Tony McAllister, Gerard Fryers, and Dermot McNally are free men.

So confident were the prison staff in the tightness of security at the Maze, that it was later revealed that strategic plans for the prison's security did not account for a breakout from within. Once the breakout was confirmed the RUC and British Army erected a cordon about one mile from the prison. Operation Vesper, it was later revealed, had been designed primarily to thwart any attempt to attack the prison from the outside.

Lord Colville caused furore among Tory government spokesmen on 25 September 1983, by saying:

> *One cannot fail to admire the competence of an organisation which enables the prisoners of war to bring to fruition an escape plan which, apart from last minute calamities, was largely successful.*

Many people up and down the country, and for that matter all around the world, held the same secret admiration for anyone who could outwit the government's prison security.

Sir James Hennessy, former chief inspector for prisons, was entrusted to compile a report on the escape. He later said:

> *I would refer to the Maze prison at the time, as being rather like Colditz during the war, in which was an impregnable fortress. For these prisoners to have got control of their block ... in a matter of twenty minutes, was absolutely staggering. I think anybody to have achieved that, must regard it as a matter of congratulation.*

One year after the escape the prison could have, once again, featured in what would have become the biggest prison breakout to have ever taken place in Ireland. At the time, the H-Blocks held almost four hundred and fifty Republican prisoners. It has been claimed that an elaborate plan was put into motion which would have led to the breakout of more than three hundred and fifty prisoners. During the September 1983 escape an incident occurred which led the organisers to realise that the main security control terminal was not as strict and as regimented as had been previously believed. The alarm had been triggered during the escape but no matter how obvious it was that something was wrong in the Tally Lodge, it soon became apparent that the emergency alarm was ignored. As things settled down after the escape, the planners eventually bribed a warder who had detailed knowledge of the workings of the Emergency Control Room. He insisted on dealing with just one man — Larry Marley. With access to such high quality information it wasn't long before the wheels went into motion and the breakout plans drawn up. Had the IRA gained control of the ECR then they would have neutralised the main link between the prison and their back-up on the outside. After taking control the prisoners would have duplicated the 1983 escape except on a larger scale. The plan was in its final stages when the warder appeared at his local police station about something unconnected with the plot. He told his interrogators the depth of his treachery and was subsequently charged and apeared in court. Had such a plan been brought to its conclusion the results on the security situation in the North would have been catastrophic.

Larry Marley was released from prison in 1985. He was shot dead at his home in Ardoyne on 2 April 1987, by the UVF. His interpretation of transportation was slightly different than that which is usually associated with Irish prisoners but it is one which shall be remembered for a long time to come.

Conclusion

The prison system, from the time of Red Hugh O'Donnell's escape to the most recent escape by Pearce McAuley and Nessan Quinlivan, has attempted over the years to become foolproof. Security procedures may have tightened, but the escapees have adapted to these new measures and merely updated their own methods of escaping. Their techniques have certainly become more innovative. There are still similarities between the first escapes and those which are happening today and common threads can be traced through many others.

Every successful escape relies, not only on the ability to break out of the confines of a prison, but also on the ability to evade recapture by one's pursuers. Like the fox escaping from the hounds it is the ability to successfully outwit the predator which counts as success.

The politics of hostage taking and the inevitable taking of prisoners in all conflict situations has been a long practised procedure. In Ireland, these procedures have been changed and adapted to every situation as it arose but the accommodation of political prisoners has had repercussions on the treatment of civilian prisoners who have, from time to time, been integrated with them due to various government policies of criminalisation and integration. Britain's penal policy, from castle dungeons to the modern day isolation units, was developed and adapted through every outpost of her empire. The development of internment camps began during the Boer War and by the time it came to introducing such measures in Ireland, they had been already tested and approved.

Internment, and the special laws which attempt to justify these measures have come in for criticism for many human rights groups across the world. Such legislation has been used by several countries, as they also try to isolate their political adversaries. These prisons and POW camps became famous throughout the world courtesy of Hollywood film makers. Their depictions of Second World War Nazi concentration camps gave credence to the duty of anyone caught up in such a scenario. The Allies attempts to escape these regimes were depicted as admirable acts of courage and fortitude. The Allied troops were not the only people faced with such a situation.

It is the sworn duty of all POWs to try to escape. If they cannot, then it is their sworn duty to cause their enemy to deploy an inordinate number of troops to guard them. On top of this it is also their sworn duty to harass their enemy to the best of their ability. This policy however in the Irish context was to be continuously debated, both by individuals caught up in the political/military situation and by the leaders within the camps and jails who had a responsibility for the safety of the men and women under their command. They also had to take into consideration the effect any escape attempt would have on the morale of the movement or whether it would set off a chain reaction of repression. The politics of escaping are carefully considered and acted upon where necessary.

All these measures were complicated further with legislation and political developments in the country itself. There were periods of internment in every generation and by 1980 remand prisoners were being held in custody for an average of eighteen months before their trial. These prisoners were faced with the chance of release at any time and any escape while on remand, or while being interned, meant a life 'on the run' or a jail term of three years, if caught, for escaping from 'lawful custody'. They were therefore being offered concessions not to escape so that everyone concerned with the running of the camps and jails would subseqently have an easy life.

There were many of the prisoners' leaders who maintained that any escape could result in a total breakdown in negotiations between themselves and governors and the relaxed regime which they enjoyed while under special category status would in turn be taken away. On the other hand, if none of the prisoners were allowed to escape then there was the possibility that any subsequent festering discontent could cause any structures which have been set up to disintegrate through insubordination.

This fact was actually encouraged by one fundamental point. The status which many prisoners and internees enjoyed which culminated in a regime similar to 'prisoners of war' was not conceded as a right but as a privilege. In effect, anyone who had status as a sentenced prisoner, relinquished that privilege upon escape or attempted escape, and, from that time, were treated as criminals and rehoused as such. Even internees, who had not been before the courts faced a prison sentence or death (as in the case of Hugh Coney in 1974) if they attempted to escape from 'lawful custody'.

Some leaders did not want to rock the boat and jeopardise any of the privileges they had, by encouraging escapes but others saw their imprisonment in a different light, and, as the Allied troops in Germany believed—if they were to be imprisoned, then the government would have to deploy extra troops and guards to watch over them and subsequently put a drain on an already hard-pressed war effort. This is, in effect, what has happened in Ireland. Even though prisons are designed to enable the least amount of guards to control an inordinate amount of prisoners. This design was ineffective once political prisoners were introduced to the system.

Following the escapes in 1971, and the findings of the Cunningham Report it was decided by the British Government to build a maximum security prison to cope with the rising prison population. This plan was revised and updated constantly as the 'Emergency' situation in the North of Ireland developed and intensified. Following a succession of escapes from jails, courts, internment camps and ships, two new prisons were built temporarily at Lisburn (Long Kesh) and Limavady (Magilligan). The 'Blocks', as they were dubbed because of their shape, immediately began to spring up adjacent to the existing camps. In the meantime a plan to build a top security prison at an old World War II airfield at Maghaberry was proposed. By the time the Gardiner Report was published in 1975, the plans had been developed with an even greater urgency. As part of his report Gardiner contended that the regimes, which by that time existed at the compounds of Long Kesh and Magilligan, resulted in the 'loss of disciplinary control' by the Prison Authorities.

Gardiner proposed the new cellular type jail system arguing that *prisons of the compound type are thoroughly unsatisfactory .... their major disadvantage is that there is virtually a total loss of control by the prison authorities inside the compounds ... discipline within the compounds is in practice exercised by compound leaders and they are more likely to emerge with an increased commitment to terrorism than as reformed citizens.*

Coupled with this development the government strengthened its contacts with other Allied governments throughout the world. This initial plan of escaping from prison and then seeking asylum in a friendly safe haven is now increasingly being challenged.

The British Government formed alliances by introducing and developing various counter-insurgency measures. The development of these international ties and the formation of extradition and criminal jurisdiction laws have meant that escapees have found it increasingly difficult to receive rights of asylum. They have succeeded in staying beyond identification and recapture by assuming new identities and merging into a new lifestyle - thus living the rest of their lives in continuous exile.

The British Government has consistently denied that there are political prisoners in Ireland and have dismissed any prisoners declaring such titles as criminal conspirators. This policy has been followed from the kidnapping of hostages such as Red Hugh O'Donnell right through the periods of internment to the present day.

The recognition of political prisoners, or prisoners of war, is quite literally in the eye of the beholder. Today's 'terrorist' may well be tomorrow's 'statesman'. Having presented the history and tradition of escapes down through the years along with the reasons and methods used, it is quite obvious that escape attempts will continue for the foreseeable future. The bottom line is, that political prisoners have consistently refused to recognise the legitimate authority of the British Government or her allies to brand them as mere criminals.

The subject of prisoners has been one of the most fundamental issues in the resolution of the conflict in Ireland. Until that conflict is resolved satisfactorily then the problem of spending millions of pounds each year trying to securely hold prisoners in jails throughout the country will remain a reality and, until then too, the escape committees will continue to prepare for their next spectacular.

Chronology of Escapes

1590   December — 1 escapes from Dublin Castle.
1592   29 December — 3 escape from Dublin Castle.

1798   3 January — 1 killed following attempt to escape from prison hulk in Belfast Lough.
1798   2 July — 1 escapes from Belfast jailhouse.
1801   29 December — 14 killed during the Hercules mutiny.
1803   December — 2 escape from Kilmainham, Dublin.

1854   2 August — 2 escape from Tasmania.
1861   25 August — 1 escapes from Van Dieman's Land.
1865   24 November — 1 escapes from Richmond Jail, Dublin.
1867   19 September — 2 escaped in Manchester, England.
1867   13 December - Attempted escape from Clerkenwell, London. 15 killed in explosion.
1869   17 February — 1 escapes from Freemantle, Western Australia.
1876   17 April — 6 prisoners escape from Freemantle, Western Australia.

1918   11 November — 1 escapes from Cork Jail.
1919   22 January — 4 escape from Usk Gaol, Wales.
1919   3 February — 3 escape from Lincoln Jail, England.
1919   16 March — 1 escapes from Mountjoy Jail, Dublin.
1919   29 March — 12 escape from Mountjoy Jail, Dublin.
1919   6 April — 1 killed while escaping from Limerick Union Hospital
1919   25 October — 6 escape from Strangeways Jail, England.

1920   June — 1 escapes from Sligo Jail
1920   30 October — 4 women escape from Moutjoy

1921   15 February — 1 escapes from Derry Jail.
1921   14 February — 3 escape from Kilmainham Jail, Dublin.
1921   29 April — 3 escape from Spike Island, Cork.
1921   9 September — 50 internees escape from Curragh Camp.
1921   22 November — 43 escape from Kilkenny prison
1921   November — 7 escape from Mountjoy Jail, Dublin.
1921   10 November — 7 escape from Spike Island, Cork.

1922   April — 1 escapes from Gormanstown Camp. (T Barry)
1922   27 July — 106 prisoners escape from Dundalk Prison.
1922   11 October — 23 escape from Courthouse in Kanturk
1922   18 October— 141 escape from Newbridge internment camp, Curragh.
1922   18 October — 10 escape from Sligo gaol

1923   October — 2 escape en route to Kilmainham

1924 16 March — 1 escapes from the Curragh Camp. (P O'Donnell)

1925 25 November — 19 escape from Mountjoy Jail, Dublin.

1926 26 February — 1 escapes from Dundrum Lunatic Asylum. (T McKeogh)

1927 9 May — 4 escaped Belfast Jail.

1941 5 June — 5 escape from Belfast Jail.
1942 Eddie Gill escapes from Peterhead.
1943 20 March — 21 escaped from Derry Jail.
1943 15 January — 4 escape from Belfast Jail.

1958 13 April — Attempt to escape from Mountjoy Jail, Dublin.
1958 24 September — 2 escape from Curragh internment camp.
1958 3 December — 16 escape from Curragh internment camp.
1959 12 February — 1 escapes from Wakefield prison, Yorkshire. (P Murphy)

1960 26 December — 1 escapes from Belfast Jail. (D Donnelly)

1966 21 February — 1 escapes from Limerick Jail. (R Behal)

1971 June — 1 escapes from Belfast Jail. (J McCann)
1971 16 July — 1 escapes from Royal Victoria Hospital, Belfast. (G Fitzgerald)
1971 9 November — 9 escape from Belfast Jail.
1971 2 December — 3 escape from Belfast Jail.

1972 7 January — 1 escapes from Palace Barracks. (F Dunlop)
1972 7 February — 1 escapes from Long Kesh dressed as a priest. (P McGuigan)
1972 17 February — 7 escape from prison ship Maidstone, Belfast Lough.
1972 18 April — 1 escapes from Musgrave Park Hospital, Belfast. (F Quigley)
1972 7 June — 1 escapes from the Mater Hospital. (Bobby Campbell)
1972 1 escaped from the Lagan Valley Hospital. (James Brown)
1972 29 October — 7 escape from Curragh.

1973 13 January — 1 escapes from Belfast Jail. (D Keenan)
1973 22 February — 1 escapes from Belfast Courthouse. (James Bryson)
1973 11 March — 1 escapes from Long Kesh. (Billy Kelly)
1973 7 April — 2 escape from Long Kesh compounds. (recaptured 3 hours later).
1973 16 August — Eamonn Campbell escaped from Altnagelvin, Derry.
1973 4 September — Billy McAllister escapes from RVH, Belfast.
1973 9 September — 1 escapes from Long Kesh dressed as a priest. (J F Greene)
1973 31 October — 3 escape from Mountjoy Jail, Dublin.
1973 8 December — 1 escapes from Long Kesh. (Brendan Hughes)
1973 12 December — 1 escapes from Belfast Jail. (G Dowdall)
1973 13 December — 1 escapes from Long Kesh compounds. (J Byrne)

1974   11 March — 1 escapes from Mountjoy. (K Littlejohn)
1974   15 April — 1escapes from Long Kesh Compounds. (Ivor Bell)
1974   8 July — 1 escapes from Long Kesh compounds. (recaptured within 3 hours)
1974   11 August — 1 escapes from RVH. (J McKee)
1974   18 August — 19 escape from Portlaoise Prison.
1974   5 November — 3 escape from Long Kesh. 1 killed.

1975   March — 1 escapes from Magilligan. (D Keenan)
1975   17 March— 1 killed during escape attempt at Portlaoise.
1975   7 May — 2 escape from Magilligan. (P O'Hagan and P McCann)
1975   19 May — 5 escape from Belfast Magistrate's Court.
1975   March — 12 escape from Newry Courthouse.
1975   20 July — 1 escapes from Long Kesh dressed as a priest. (P Campbell)
1975   14 August — 2 escape from Curragh Military Hospital.

1976   1 escapes from Magilligan. (M Monaghan)
1976   5 May — 8 escape from Long Kesh compounds

1977   15 July — 4 escape from Green Street Special Court .
(3 captured immediately)(M O'Rourke)

1980   16 December — 1 escapes from Brixton with the help of two other prisoners.

1981   10 June — 8 escape from Belfast Jail.

1983   25 September — 38 escape from Maze.

1991   7 July — 2 escaped from Brixton Prison, London.

1994   9 September — Attempted escape of 5 republicans from Whitemoor prison, Cambridgeshire.

1995   20 November — attempted to escape from Musgrave Park hospital.

Index

G

H

M

N

BIBLIOGRAPHY

As I Roved Out. Cathal O'Byrne. Blackstaff Press. Belfast. 1982

Ballymurphy and the Irish War. Cíarán de Baróid. Pluto Press. London 1990

Belfast Graves Vols.1 and 2. The National Graves Association. AP/RN Print Dublin 1985 and 1994

Cage 11. Gerry Adams. Brandon Book Publishers Ltd. Co. Kerry. 1990

Derry Jail. Colm Cavanagh. Guildhall Press. Derry. 1982

Éalú ón gCaisleán. Cliodna Cussen. Oifig an tSoláthair, Baile Átha Cliath. 1978

Freemantle Mission. Seán Ó Lúng. Anvil Books Ltd. Tralee. 1965

Géarchéim in Éirinn. Dick Walsh. Foilseacháin Náisiúta Teoranta, Báile Átha Cliath. 1970

Kilmainham, The Bastille of Ireland. The Kilmainham Jail Restoration Society. Dublin 1982

Leaves from the diary of Nurse Linda Kearns. Edited by Annie M P Smithson. Dublin 1922.

On another Man's Wounds. Ernie O'Malley. Anvil. Dublin 1978

Out of the Maze. Derek Dunne. Gill And Macmillan Ltd. Dublin 1988.

Selected poems, speeches, dedications and letters of John Boyle O'Reilly. Liam Barry. The National Gaelic Publications, Australind, Western Australia 1994.

Survivors. Uinseann Mac Eoin. Argenta Publications, Dublin 1987

Sworn to be Free. Florence O'Donoghue. Anvil Books Ltd. Kerry 1971

The Cause of Ireland. Liz Curtis. Out of the Pale. Belfast 1995

The Convict Ships. Charles Bateson. Brown Son & Ferguson, Ltd. Glasgow 1959.

The INLA. Henry McDonald and Jack Holand. Torc. Dublin 1994

The IRA. Tim Pat Coogan. Fontana/Collins. Galsgow 1987

The History of Belfast. George Benn

The Secret Army. J Boyer Bell. Poolbeg Ltd. Dublin 1978

The Singing Flame. Ernie O'Malley. Anvil. Dublin 1978

The Town Book of Belfast. R M Young. Marcus Ward & Co Ltd. Belfast 1892

The Troubles; Ireland's Ordeal 1966-1995 and the search for peace. Tim Pat Coogan. Hutchinson. London 1995.

Periodicals and journals
An Phoblacht
An Phoblacht / Republican News
Derry Journal
Iris Autumn 1993 Edition

The Belfast Bulletin No.10. Worker's Research Unit
The Belfast News-Letter
The Belfast Telegraph
The Freeman's Journal
The FreemantleHerald
The Irish Independant
The Irish News
The Irish Times
The Irishman
The Northern Star
The Weekly Northern Whig

If you enjoyed this book, you may also enjoy

NOTHING BUT THE SAME OLD STORY
by Liz Curtis

ISBN 1 901005 00 3

PRICE £4.50 stg + p&p

Nothing But The Same Old Story was first published by Information on Ireland in 1984 with support from the then Greater London Council, as part of its anti-racism campaign. The book was very well received and rapidly became a classic.

It is now reprinted by Sásta, a voluntary publishing group based in Belfast. If you would like details of our other publications, send a stamped addressed envelope to: Sásta, The Ashton Centre, 5 Churchill Street, Belfast BT15 2BP